# John Gould's Birds

# John Gould's Birds

CHARTWELL
BOOKS, INC.

Published by
**CHARTWELL BOOKS, INC.**
A Division of **BOOK SALES, INC.**
110 Enterprise Avenue
Secaucus, New Jersey 07094

Maureen Lambourne was brought up in Belfast. After taking a
degree in Fine Art at Reading University, she worked at the
Victoria and Albert Museum for eight years in the departments of
Ceramics and Prints and Drawings. She gave adult education
lectures on the Applied Arts in Leicester. Maureen Lambourne has
written several articles on her great-great-grandfather John Gould
and other animal artists for *Country Life* and other journals.

Scientific Adviser: Silvio Pirovano
Editor: Mariella de Battisti
Editorial Assistants: Paola Lovato, Marisa Melis
Art Editor: Enrico Segré
© Copyright 1980 Arnoldo Mondadori Editore, Milan
Based on John Gould *Die Vögel Grossbritanniens* © copyright 1979
Harenberg Kommunikation, Dortmund
English text © copyright 1980 Arnoldo Mondadori Editore,
Milan

First published in the United States of America in 1981 by
A & W Publishers, Inc.
95 Madison Avenue
New York, New York 10016

Library of Congress Catalog Card Number: 81-66211
ISBN: 0-89479-088-9

Originally published in Italian under the title
*Gli Uccelli di John Gould*

Filmset by Keyspools Ltd., Golborne, Lancs.
Printed and bound in Spain
by Artes Graficas Toledo S.A.
D. L. TO:834-1987

# Contents

John Gould: the Bird Man                                                                    7
by Maureen Lambourne

Raptores (Birds of Prey and Owls)                                                          33

Insessores (Nightjars, Swifts, Kingfishers and their Allies, and Perching Birds)          55

Insessores (Perching Birds, Cuckoos, and Woodpeckers)                                      97

Rasores (Pigeons and their Allies, Gallinaceous Birds, and Bustards) and                  139
    Grallatores (Cranes, Herons and their Allies, Waders, and Rails)

Natatores (Waterfowl and Sea Birds)                                                        187

Systematic Index of the Species Illustrated                                                233

Index of Illustrations                                                                     236

Bibliography                                                                               239

A water-colour portrait of John Gould
by Miss Walker (1875) (Natural
History Museum, London).

# John Gould:
## The Bird Man

John Gould was born on September 14, 1804, at Lyme Regis, Dorset. This small coastal town, with a population of 1,451 in 1801, was a quiet but thriving fashionable resort. It was recommended by doctors for its wonderful air and the safety of its bathing in the southerly sheltered bay. In the season, bathing machines were dotted about in the water and visitors would promenade along the Cobb, an old stone pier dating from the fourteenth century.

For a description of the fashionable aspect of Lyme, no words could be more apt than those of Jane Austen who stayed there in the autumn of 1804, the year of Gould's birth. Jane Austen immortalized her stay in *Persuasion* where she describes the visit paid by Anne Elliot and her friends. The young people, who were 'all wild to see Lyme', went to the sands to watch the flowing of the tide. 'They praised the morning; gloried in the sea; sympathized in the delight of the fresh-feeling breeze—and were silent; till Henrietta suddenly began with "Oh! yes,—I am quite convinced that, with very few exceptions, the sea-air always does good."'

This delight in the outdoor world, which Jane Austen portrays as a light-hearted whim, had grander and more serious implications. An emotional involvement with nature appears in the Romantic poetry of Wordsworth, Shelley, and Keats. Wordsworth in particular voiced contemporary thought in the descriptions of his intense feelings for the beauty of the roar of a waterfall, of a wood of daffodils, a bunch of snowdrops, or the song of a lark. Childhood memories of pure enjoyment are often recollected by Wordsworth; and *The Sparrow's Nest* seems to foretell an experience John Gould describes. As a child John Gould's father lifted him up to see the vivid blue eggs in a sparrow's nest in their garden:

> Behold, within the leafy shade,
> Those bright blue eggs together laid!
> On me the chance-discovered sight
> Gleamed like a vision of delight

In his introduction to the *Birds of Great Britain*, Gould wrote that from this first moment he 'became enamoured with nature, and her charming attitudes; it was then I received an impulse which has not only never lost its influence, but which has gone on acquiring new force through a long life.' Gould's insatiable curiosity and restless enthusiasm were to result in his publications on the birds and animals of three continents, monographs on the toucans, trogons, and humming-birds, illustrations to two ships' voyages, and about 300 scientific articles and papers.

Regrettably little is known of John Gould's antecedents and family background. His father, John Gould, born in 1783, was a gardener, and came from a large family. Young John Gould seems to have had one brother and one or two sisters. When he was still a child, his father moved to Stoke Hill, near Guildford, Surrey. It was in this fertile Surrey countryside, with its great variety of meadow, woodland, pond and riverside, that Gould made his early discoveries, for this area is rich in wild life. Writing in old age, Gould recalled 'the associations of my boyhood ever flitting before me', and described in the *Birds of Great Britain* how, in spring, he and his friends collected 'particoloured strings of eggs' with which 'they delighted to festoon the walls' but 'which were rigorously destroyed in our games before the end of the year'. He also remembered the superstitions of the cottagers, how, from their ceiling, they would hang a dried kingfisher whose movements were then said to point the direction of the wind. However, he often felt that the country folk, in spite of the richness of bird life around them, knew little of bird nomenclature or habits.

The descriptions of Gould's avid collecting of birds' nests and the shooting of birds for specimens may seem deplorable to us today. At that time, however, there was little concern for conservation and the Wild Birds Protection Act was not passed until 1880. But in his writings Gould often showed an awareness of the need to protect certain species such as the waxwing or the osprey.

It is not known where Gould went to school, or the extent of his education. However, he did have a feeling for the English language, for later he was to write in a fine style, fluently and forcefully, though sometimes rather ponderously and rhetorically. His text often included quotations and allusions to classical and English literature, as was the manner of the time.

## 2. THE GARDENER

The Gould family moved to Windsor, in 1818, and finally settled there, as Gould's father was appointed a gardener in the Royal Gardens. Windsor Castle, inhabited by the aged George III, was then a straggling and comfortless building; it was later transformed by Sir Jeffry Wyatville, architect to his son, George IV, into a flamboyant palace, with a romantic skyline of round towers and crenellated walls. Then, however, the ghostly King Lear-like figure of the mad monarch could sometimes be seen at the window of the North Terrace, during the ceremony of the changing of the guard.

In the Great Park, Gould would have seen the herd of deer, and have been taken to the Royal Menagerie of animals at Sandpit Gate.

When he was fourteen years old, Gould was placed under the care of Mr Aiken, the head gardener, to learn the same trade as his father. One of his tasks, as he recalled in old age to his friend and biographer, Dr Richard Bowdler Sharpe, was to pick 'many a bunch of dandelion leaves' for the elderly Queen Charlotte's favourite dandelion tea. The royal couple had often been caricatured for their domestic frugality, and it is amusing to think that perhaps dandelion tea was one of the royal economies.

The Gould association with the Royal Family lasted into Queen Victoria's time, for John Gould's daughter recalls how, when she was a child, every Christmas Grandmother Gould would send from Windsor to London a hamper of good things, including 'pretty things from the Christmas tree at Windsor Castle which she got by favour'.

During this time, Gould became skilled in the art of taxidermy. The British Museum's zoology collection, now at Tring, Hertfordshire, still possesses a couple of magpies shot and set up by Gould when he was only fourteen. In his spare time, Gould supplied stuffed birds to the boys at Eton, the famous public school near Windsor. His skill at egg-blowing was also in demand—the eggs may well have been used for the childhood games Gould later recalled, or placed carefully in cabinets for decoration and study.

Gould's first appointment as a gardener was at Ripley Castle, Yorkshire, owned by Sir William Ingilby. The castle had belonged to the Ingilby family since the fourteenth century, but Sir William Ingilby, an eccentric, had great plans to rebuild the castle on continental lines—the village was to be based on buildings in Alsace-Lorraine, and the castle became referred to as the Schloss. These changes took place after Gould's stay, but he may have seen the building of the first cottages which were set off by trees and broad grass verges.

Gould spent only a short time in Yorkshire, and, by about 1825, he came south again, this time to London, where he abandoned his gardener's career and set up a business as a taxidermist.

An engraving (1848) by T.H. Maguire, which shows John Gould at the age of forty-five.

### 3. TAXIDERMY

Taxidermy, the art of preparing and mounting skins of animals in a lifelike manner, had become a commercial proposition in England in the early nineteenth century. New skins were continually arriving from abroad for classification and owners wished to preserve the exotic creatures which had died in their zoos and menageries.

Attempts had been made since the seventeenth century to stuff specimens but almost nothing has survived from these times. The first collections, such as the mounted birds given to the British Museum by Sir Hans Sloane, in 1753, and the specimens from the Captain Cook voyages from 1768 to 1771, all seem to have disintegrated. A rare survivor is the grey parrot, in the crypt of Westminster Abbey, London, whose owner 'La Belle Stuart', one of Charles II's mistresses and the model for Britannia on English coins, requested that her parrot be placed beside her wax effigy after her death in 1702.

The early methods of taxidermy were rather crude, as shown in a pamphlet, *Short directions for collecting, preserving and transporting all kinds of Natural History Curiosities*, by Johann Reinhold Forster in 1771. To preserve a bird, the entrails, lungs and craw were removed. It was then washed with a liquid containing arsenic and dried with a powder mixture of tobacco sand, black pepper, burnt alum and arsenic. The body was stuffed with tow, the eyes replaced with painted putty, and it was dried in an oven. As probably too much flesh was still left in the body, the preservative used could have had little effect, and it soon decayed or was attacked by insects.

Continental workers, especially the French, were ahead of the British in the eighteenth and early nineteenth centuries, but by the 1820s the recipe for French arsenic soap was being used in England. William Swainson in 1840 described a mixture of camphor, arsenic, soap, salt of tartar, and chalk, which could be made into soap cakes or paste. He emphasized that great care had to be taken to make sure that the fingers and finger nails were well washed afterwards, otherwise sore fingers would result!

As the century advanced, very realistic and more elaborate groups were mounted and it became the fashion to display these in glass cases or shades as interior decoration. An enormous case of humming-birds, artistically and gracefully arranged as a Victorian display, is on view at the Natural History Museum, London, and, though faded, gives some idea of the splendid, shimmering, glittering effect that hundreds of these tiny creatures would have.

Gould did not contribute to the anthropomorphic tableaux of stuffed animals which portrayed stories such as Walter Potter's *Death and Burial of Cock Robin*, completed in 1861, in which the Sussex taxidermist used specimens of British birds. Gould remained a dedicated ornithologist, but the artistic ability which he developed in displaying and mounting specimens proved to be the basis of his skill in planning and designing the plates for his books.

Caricature entitled *The Camelopard or a New Hobby* (1827) (London, British Museum). This portrays King George IV and Lady Conyngham riding the giraffe given to the sovereign by Mehemet Ali of Egypt.

Caricature by William Heath entitled *The State of the Giraffe* (Victoria and Albert Museum, London).

## 4. CURATOR AND PRESERVER

Soon after Gould's return to London, an event took place which was to be of fundamental importance to his career. This was the formation of the Zoological Society of London. The society was founded on April 29, 1826, at a general meeting and Sir Stamford Raffles was elected President. The society was first conceived as an offshoot of the Linnaean Society, founded in 1788 and mostly concerned with botany, and was instituted to 'promote zoological knowledge'. Its aims were to 'form a collection of living animals, a museum of preserved animals, with a collection of comparative anatomy, and a library concerned with the subject'. A house, 33 Bruton Street, was taken for offices and a museum, and a site at Regent's Park for the live exhibits.

In 1827, John Gould was appointed 'Curator and Preserver to the Museum'. There were already 450 specimens, enough to justify a catalogue. Many of these, including a clouded tiger, were donated by Sir Stamford Raffles, who had travelled widely in the Far East and India, and others were given by Captain (later Sir John) Franklin and Captain Parry after an Arctic expedition. A number of live animals were temporarily housed in the museum, such as a wanderloo monkey, described as a 'right merry fellow' who caused much mischief and was unjustly accused of destroying a book of vouchers.

At this period Gould stuffed mammals as well as birds, and there survive accounts of his work for the Royal Family. On May 20, 1826, Gould was paid £3.0.0 by George IV for 'Preserving his Mouse Deer', and £10.10.0 for 'Preserving and Caseing an Ostrich'. The following year £41.12.0 was paid for 'Stuffing Birds by His Majesty's Order'. In 1828 Gould again stuffed an ostrich, this time for £7.0.0, and also an emu, horse, roe, gazelle and chamois for £5.0.0 each, a monkey for £2.0.0, and a king vulture for £1.10.0. From the last full year of George IV's reign, 1829, an account for £1.5.0 survives for preserving a 'Thick Knee'd Bustard'. These animals presumably came from the Royal Menagerie, one of George IV's enthusiasms.

## 5. THE GIRAFFE

The largest and most exciting commission Gould received was to stuff George IV's prized giraffe. This poor animal, the first live giraffe to be seen in England, was a present from Mehemet Ali of Egypt and had travelled across the desert strapped to the back of a camel. It arrived at Waterloo Bridge, London, in August 1827, and was then taken to Windsor Great Park.

The King's attachment to the giraffe was seized on by caricaturists as an example of his extravagant and outré taste. One caricature, *The Camelopard or a New Hobby*, shows the giraffe carrying the obese George IV and his bulky mistress Lady Conyngham.

Unfortunately the giraffe's legs never fully recovered from its journey from Africa, and William Heath's caricature *The State of the Giraffe* shows the enfeebled animal being raised by a pulley turned by the King and Lady Conyngham. A small note in the margin adds the remark, 'I suppose we shall have to pay for stuffing him next.'

The giraffe died about two years after its arrival, and the *Windsor and Eton Express*, October 17, 1829, stated: 'Messrs. Gould and Tomkins of the Zoological Gardens are now dissecting the Giraffe which expired on Sunday last. We understand that when the skin is stuffed, His Majesty intends making it a present to the Zoological Society.'

The skin and skeleton were given to the Zoo's collection by George's successor William IV. It could be seen 'beautifully prepared' until about 1855, when the collection was disbanded and most exhibits entered the Natural History Museum. The giraffe, however, was purchased by a Dr Crisp. Its whereabouts today are unknown.

## 6. MARRIAGE

With a successful career in taxidermy and zoological research assured him, Gould, now aged twenty-four, was able to marry. He was to be singularly fortunate in his choice of partner. On January 5, 1829, at St James's Church, Piccadilly, he married Elizabeth Coxen. 'All who spoke of her said she was incredibly sweet looking, a good and accomplished woman, and an affectionate wife and mother.' So wrote her eldest daughter, Eliza Gould, who was only five years old when her mother died. However, all other accounts also describe Elizabeth Gould as considerate, charming and cultured.

Portrait of Elizabeth Coxen, John Gould's wife (Private Collection, England).

Elizabeth's gentle manners no doubt played their part in giving Gould some much needed social poise. This was to be vitally important to him, for much of his future career was to be passed in learned societies, distinguished clubs like the Athenaeum, and in aristocratic circles amongst whose members he was to find the wealthy subscribers for his books. His ebullient temperament and outward joviality enabled him to pass, for example, an evening in March 1841, at Lord Northampton's home, entertaining the company, including Albert, the Prince Consort, with his pretty singing New South Wales parrots. But his business methods remained brusque and direct, and he never seems to have acquired the finesse of a gentleman.

Elizabeth Gould was born at Ramsgate on July 18, 1804, two months before her husband-to-be, of a family with military and naval connections. At the time of her marriage, she was the only child, of a family of nine, left in England; the two other surviving children, her brothers Stephen and Charles Coxen, had emigrated to Australia.

A rather sad, homesick letter to her mother from James Street, Buckingham Palace, London, shows that Elizabeth was a governess before she met John Gould. She writes that she is going to teach her nine-year-old pupil French, Latin, and music. Her room overlooked the Palace and barracks and 'were it not that I see constantly *living* things *really* moving backwards and forwards there, I should fancy I was to be shut up here for ever without knowing anyone who could enter into one's feelings.' She seemed worried that she would have no opportunity to meet society: 'I feel I shall get very melancholy here,' she wrote, and with further anxiety added, 'I know not what it may be in the summer.'

There is no surviving account of how she met John Gould, but it was probably during a visit, perhaps a sketching trip, to the Zoo, for the Gardens and Museum were open to the public from April 1828, if the visitor had the written permission of a Fellow of the Society. Certainly after she met the young curator, her life took a dramatic turn, for in place of a lonely existence in a cloistered house, she was, in twelve years of marriage, to present her husband with six children, help him with at least 600 bird illustrations, and travel to Australia and back.

In the year after their marriage Gould acquired a collection, from some unknown source, of bird skins from the hill countries of the Himalayas. These valuable specimens had not been seen in England before, and when Gould had stuffed and mounted them, he saw their artistic qualities and visualized how well they would look in an illustrated book.

For inspiration on how this project was to be achieved he would have turned to the bird books that were then available or in production.

## 7. JOHN JAMES AUDUBON

The most spectacular of the bird books then in production was John James Audubon's *Birds of America* (1827–38). It was composed of monumental double elephant-sized folios (75cm × 1m) which had plates beautifully engraved on metal and hand-coloured by William

John James Audubon: Mallards in a swamp.

Lizars of Edinburgh, who produced the first ten plates, and Robert Havell of London.

John James Audubon, born on April 26, 1785, in Haiti, the illegitimate son of Jean Audubon, a French merchant seaman, and Mlle Rabin, a Creole from San Domingo, was brought up in France but emigrated to his father's farm at Mill Grove near Philadelphia when he was eighteen years old. Although he made several attempts to enter commerce, his ventures met with failure and bankruptcy, and he turned away from business life to spend many years seeking and drawing birds, whilst living on what he could earn as an artist and ornithologist.

He set sail for England on May 17, 1826, with the purpose of finding a publisher for his bird illustrations. In Liverpool and in Edinburgh his work and personality aroused great curiosity and wonder. Nicknamed 'The American Woodsman', because of his romantic appearance—shoulder-length chestnut ringlets and fringed buckskin jacket—Audubon was wined and dined by one institution after another.

In May 1827 Audubon proceeded to London, and he described in a letter how on the evening of June 22, he opened his portfolios 'before a set of learned men and they saw many birds they had not dreamed of. Charles [Bonaparte, the Emperor's nephew and a well-known ornithologist] offered to name them for me, and I felt happy that he should; and with a pencil he actually christened upwards of fifty, urging me to publish them at once in manuscript at the Zoological

Society.' John Gould may not have been then sufficiently learned to be present on this historic occasion, but later he bought some of Audubon's prints. In a letter to Robert Havell, September 1830, Audubon wrote that Gould 'may have a Sett uncoloured for 30 shillings a number—the Price I sold one at Manchester, and you must see that he pays you cash down, as I fear he is not over and above able to purchase such a work on credit'.

Audubon, unlike other ornithologists of the time, had received training as an artist. On several occasions he stated that he had studied in the atelier of the great French master Jacques-Louis David, in Paris, and in America he had earned his living as a professional portrait painter. For his magnificent bird studies he used a combination of pencil, pastel, ink, oil, and egg-white. In order to capture the living likeness of a bird with its fresh colouring, Audubon used a unique method; he set up his recently killed models in positions secured by wires which pierced their wings, head, and body. Thus he avoided the necessity of stuffing the model, painting from the faded specimen, or being forced to show his subject in one stereotyped position.

Audubon's explorations through eastern America, particularly along the Ohio and Mississippi rivers, provided him with birds which he recorded in their natural habitat with an animation hitherto unknown in any illustrator's work. Sometimes his dynamic compositions became almost frenzied and scientists questioned their accuracy, such as the rattlesnake climbing up a tree towards a frightened mocking bird.

The expense of engraving elaborate plates for these double elephant folios was immense and therefore the price of a set (435 prints) staggering—$1,000. It is hence not surprising that Audubon spent a great deal of precious time searching for subscribers and persuading them to pay.

On his later visits to London, Audubon must have met Gould many times, although a specific occasion has not been recorded. Audubon borrowed skins from Gould, such as the horned puffin, which the former had not been able to draw from life. In a letter of April 20, 1835, to his friend John Bachman in America, Audubon mentions that he had acquired a dog from Gould to send him: 'By way of Dogs—I also forward you a Pointer Bitch of finest English Blood—I call her most beautiful—She is perfect as a Pointer and you can easily keep up the breed. I received her from Mr. Gould, the naturalist. Her value here is £20—she is 5 years old. Her name is Belle.' Belle safely arrived at her destination in Charleston, South Carolina, and later Audubon sent a dog from the Earl of Derby to join her.

Although the names of Audubon and Gould have often been linked as the finest bird book publishers of the nineteenth century, their manner of illustration was very different. It is interesting to compare a few of the birds they both depicted. There are, for example, Audubon's pintail ducks, whose necks crane upwards eager to catch a moth, whereas Gould's ducks are quietly waddling towards the water. Audubon's great white heron strides forward with a fish in its bill, Gould's pair of herons are perched side by side in a tree. Audubon's great black-backed gull lies bleeding, its wing shattered by a storm, whereas Gould's gull glides peacefully through the water. Allan McEvey, the Australian scholar, brilliantly sums up their different styles. 'While Audubon's appeal is spectacular and striking, that of a Gould print grows quietly upon us. It is the appeal of the chaste and formal which, especially in the smaller birds, attains the lyrical. At its best its union of science and art is permanently satisfying.'

## 8. OTHER BIRD ILLUSTRATORS: THOMAS BEWICK, WILLIAM SWAINSON AND BENJAMIN WATERHOUSE HAWKINS

During his stay in England, Audubon travelled to the north-east county of Northumberland, to see the wood-engraver and naturalist, Thomas Bewick, whose books he much enjoyed. He described Bewick as 'a son of Nature' and 'a perfect old English gentleman, full of life, although seventy-four years of age, active and prompt in all his labours'. Bewick's classic work, *A History of British Birds* (1797–1804), was illustrated by small wood-engravings with the portrait of a bird as the heading of a page and a vignette of a country scene as the tailpiece. The technique of engraving on these small blocks of box wood was quite unique, for Bewick could convey rain or snow, riverside grasses or woodland plants, even the texture of feathers, by exposing the grain of the wood and cutting it with fine, delicate lines. Gould expressed his admiration for Bewick in his introduction to the *Birds of Great Britain*, and his own plates of everyday birds such as the robin, sparrow, or owl are often very similar in conception, though very different in scale and technique.

Audubon's engraver for the first ten plates of the *Birds of America*, William Lizars, also produced plates for John Selby's *Illustrations of British Ornithology*, the first parts appearing in 1823. These fine, hand-coloured copper engravings, larger in format than Gould's folio volumes, of life-size birds, were very much overshadowed by Audubon's work and are now seldom reproduced. Gould must have been impressed by their fine quality, but realized that the engraving technique was slow and expensive and experienced craftsmen difficult to find.

Another book published in the early nineteenth century was William Swainson's *Zoological Illustrations* (1820–23). This was smaller in format and contained beautifully hand-coloured lithographs of foreign birds. Particularly attractive were the kingfishers with their brilliant blue colouring. Swainson was a pioneer in his use of lithography, and the slightly stiff attitudes of his birds remind one of metal engravings, but nevertheless the whole effect is one of great charm and delicacy.

A successor to Swainson's *Zoological Illustrations* was J. E. Gray and Thomas Hardwicke's *Illustrations of India Zoology* (1830–34). This book illustrated Major-General Hardwicke's collection of Indian birds and animals gathered when he served in the military service of the Honourable East India Company. He had employed a native artist to do the drawings and Benjamin Waterhouse Hawkins lithographed the plates.

These included a miscellany of creatures—a hedgehog, a gerboa rat, vultures, owls, pheasants, a fighting cock, woodpeckers, a bird of paradise, terrapins, toads, and fish. The Indian pheasants are remarkably like the illustrations in Gould's *A Century of Birds from the Himalaya Mountains*—sparse, simple, outlines coloured in brown and reds. Waterhouse Hawkins was a fine draughtsman and captured the individual characters of these very diverse subjects.

The East India Company was the main subscriber to this book, but the Linnaean Society also purchased a copy, and Gould may have seen it in the library. These lithographs of Indian birds were perhaps a direct influence on his new project, especially as the book appeared in parts from 1830, just at the time when Gould was looking for advice. Waterhouse Hawkins featured later in Gould's life, as contributor of one plate to the *Birds of Australia*, lithographer of Gould's plates for the *Zoology of the H.M.S. Sulphur*, and host at an amusing dinner party described later.

## 9. EDWARD LEAR'S 'PARROTS'

The work of the modest and sensitive Edward Lear provided further inspiration for Gould when embarking on his first project, *A Century of Birds from the Himalaya Mountains*.

Edward Lear, born in 1812, and thus eight years younger than Gould, was the youngest of twenty-one children, and brought up chiefly by his eldest sister, since their father had been ruined by financial speculation and the family had had to leave their fine house in Holloway, North London. At the age of fifteen, lack of money and ill health had forced Lear into the hack work of colouring screens and fans and tinting medical plates illustrating diseases. In an attempt to escape this repetitive drudgery, Lear at the age of eighteen started to produce, at his own expense, *The Family of the Psittacidae*, a book of forty-two hand-coloured lithographs of parrots mostly drawn from life. He obtained permission from the Zoological Society to make drawings, and Gould must have met the young artist at the Gardens, or at Bruton Street, where the parrots were housed until the aviary was completed.

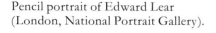

Pencil portrait of Edward Lear (London, National Portrait Gallery).

Unfortunately for Lear, although the book contains magnificently impressive plates, it was not a financial success. The cost of paying a colourist and printer for the limited edition of 175 copies, and the difficulties of getting the subscribers to pay, forced him to abandon the project after the twelfth folio. Lear had originally planned to portray all the parrot family then known.

In 1834, two years later, Gould wrote to Sir William Jardine that he had purchased from Lear the remainder of his stock, with the idea of finishing the work himself, but this plan was not carried out.

## 10. LITHOGRAPHY

Edward Lear, Benjamin Waterhouse Hawkins, and William Swainson used the recently discovered method of lithography for their prints, and this novel process, easily workable and thus profitable, was to lead to Gould's many successful publications.

The process of lithography is a simple one. It was the first surface or planographic process discovered, and thus differed from previous printing processes which were intaglio or engraved.

Lithograph of a yellow and blue parrot by Edward Lear (London, Victoria and Albert Museum).

Lithographic printers used large slabs of limestone, about 55 cms by 40 cms, a convenient folio book size. The artist drew his picture, such as the outline of a bird, on the stone with a special black greasy chalk or pencil. In the early days of lithography, the drawing was done in reverse, so that the print would turn out the right way round, but later tracing paper was used. The stone was then washed with a light etch, or nitric acid solution, which opened up the pores of the stone so it could be successfully sealed with a coat of gum arabic. The printer damped the stone with water and rolled on special greasy ink which stuck only to the chalk drawing. Paper was placed on top, and the whole passed through a printing press. The result was a clear printed outline, ready to be coloured by hand.

The great advantage of the process was that the artist could draw his picture on the stone in chalk with a cursive, flexible line, and with a little practice was soon able to produce a satisfactory result. The technical ability and skill needed for engraving with tools on to the rigid metal plate or wooden block was thus avoided. The prints, too, when hand-coloured, had the soft, realistic qualities of a water-colour painting, very different from the hard, wiry line of a metal engraving or the strong grain of a print from wood.

Lithography was invented by Aloys Senefelder in Munich, in 1798, after many years of experiment. Senefelder led an itinerant life, travelling through Europe with his printing discoveries. In 1801 he established a printing business in London with Philip André, but little interest was taken in this new graphic art. Some years later, in 1818, Charles Hullmandel, who had studied the process with Senefelder in Munich, published *Twenty-four views of Italy* and founded his own shop in London the next year. Also in 1819, the print-sellers firm Ackermanns published an English edition of Senefelder's book, *A Complete Course of Lithography*. A new interest in lithography developed, and famous artists, such as the French Romantic painter, Théodore Géricault, used Hullmandel's printing shop. James Ward, an English Romantic painter of animals, made a series of fourteen

Two shrikes – male above and female below – drawn from life by Elizabeth Gould for *A Century of Birds from the Himalaya Mountains* (1831–1832).

lithographs, *Celebrated Horses* (1823–24).

Charles Hullmandel printed Edward Lear's *Book of Parrots*, and he was later to be of invaluable help to John Gould. His firm printed the majority of his 2,999 plates. After Charles Hullmandel's death in 1850, Gould also employed other firms, such as Walter and Cohn who printed the *Birds of Great Britain*. It was indeed fortunate that Gould could turn to such a capable craftsman to print his first book, *A Century of Birds from the Himalaya Mountains* (1831–32).

## 11. THE BIRDS OF THE HIMALAYAS

John Gould was not to be daunted by his lack of experience as an artist or lithographer in proceeding with the production of his book. Dr Bowdler Sharpe, in his biography, describes how Gould introduced the subject to his wife, Elizabeth: 'But who will do the plates on stone?' she asked. 'Who?' replied her husband. 'Why, you, of course.'

Elizabeth Gould was a talented artist and the art of sketching and plant drawing was one of her accomplishments as a governess. She soon learned, though tentatively at first, how to draw directly on stone, producing the figures for over a hundred birds on eighty plates, each of which bear the inscription, 'Drawn from Nature and on Stone by E. Gould'. 'From Nature' meant from the mounted specimen and not the live model. The birds are placed very simply on tree stumps or branches, presumably because Gould was unable to supply a Himalayan background, and have a simplicity and starkness quite different from later, more elaborate productions.

Now that Gould had found a printer and an artist, he sought an expert to assist him in the scientific descriptions of the birds and the text. He gained the advice of Nicholas Vigors, then secretary of the Zoological Society, who named a previously unrecorded tiny multi-coloured sunbird *Aethyopyga Gouldiae* in honour of Elizabeth Gould. Gould had decided to be his own publisher, and his final task now was to find subscribers, for at least 200 were needed to launch a book of this type and achieve financial success.

In this respect Gould showed great business acumen. His subscription list was headed by King William iv and Queen Adelaide to whom he dedicated the book, and followed by various earls, dukes, and lords. These gentlemen had their own country estates and menageries with collections of exotic animals, and libraries, where the large folio books when bound would look very impressive. Other subscribers were institutions and societies and also natural historians such as Dr Ruppell of Frankfurt, Baron Cuvier of Paris, Sir William Jardine, and John Selby. Artists like Lear and Audubon probably exchanged their own work for a copy. Gould found 298 subscribers and the venture made a huge profit, paving the way for the enormous success of future productions.

Trogon, drawn from life by Elizabeth Gould for John Gould's monograph on the Trogons (1838).

In Gould's prospectus of January 1, 1866, he listed all his subscribers who amounted to the grand total of 1,008, including twelve monarchs, sixteen dukes, six marquises, thirty earls, five counts, ten viscounts, one bishop, and thirty-six lords. The most popular books were the *Birds of Great Britain*, with 397 subscribers, who each paid £78.15.0 for a set, and the *Birds of Australia* the most expensive series, costing £115. Most of the books were issued in separate parts, each costing £3.0.0, a figure only the wealthy could afford.

We can sympathize with Gould's friend, William Swainson, who expressed a hope that was never fulfilled, in his *Biography of Zoologists* (1840): 'John Gould:—A zealous, and very able ornithologist, now travelling in Australia, who has published some valuable though very expensive works on birds. We trust the author will hereafter reprint these expensive volumes in such a form as they may be accessible to naturalists: and thereby diffuse science, instead of restricting it to those only who are wealthy.'

## 12. THE BIRDS OF EUROPE

After the success of *A Century of Birds from the Himalaya Mountains*, Gould decided to illustrate birds nearer home. The *Birds of Europe* (1832–1837) was of greater general appeal and the plates were more artistically composed, with the birds delicately placed on sprays or amongst plants which formed a simple, coloured background.

Gould was now able to organize a team of workers to ensure the steady production of illustrations. He himself was continually active in obtaining specimens and information, and, through his Zoological Society contacts, wrote to scholars abroad and visited the zoos and museums of Holland, Germany, and Switzerland. Audubon described the Goulds at work in a letter to John Bachman, 1836: 'Gould is a man of great industry—he has the advantage of the Zoological Society's Museums, Gardens, etc. and is in correspondence with Temminck, Jardine, Selby, James Wilson and the rest of Scientific Gentry—his *Wife* makes his drawings on stone. She is a plain, fine, woman, and although these Works are not quite up to Nature, both deserve great credit.'

The plates were based on rough drawings which Gould himself made of the mounted models. These were bold pencil or charcoal sketches, indicating the position of the birds on the page, plants to be used, and annotated with remarks and sometimes dabs of colour. Elizabeth Gould modelled her drawings on stone on these sketches; she also prepared plant drawings and water-colours of the birds as a guide for the colourists. Her plates bore the inscription, 'J. & E. Gould del et lith', the conventional method of indicating that the plates were drawn and lithographed by John and Elizabeth Gould.

To assist his wife, Gould employed Edward Lear who had now given up his book on parrots. Lear illustrated the larger birds, such as the owl, vulture, purple heron, whistling swan, pelican, and great auk. His owls seem particularly formidable, immobile on simple branches, their large looming eyes are almost hypnotic, in contrast to Elizabeth Gould's graceful birds set amongst carefully drawn plants. Lear's purple heron and demoiselle crane stand gaunt and statuesque, and the huge whistling swan and dalmatian pelican dominate the page with their great bodies, large webbed feet and curved necks.

Two very colourful monographs, the *Toucans* and the *Trogons*, illustrated by Elizabeth Gould and Edward Lear followed the *Birds of Europe*. Lear had meanwhile, in 1832, received an invitation from the Earl of Derby to his country house, Knowsley Hall, to illustrate *Gleanings from the Menagerie and Aviary at Knowsley Hall*. It was here, amongst the elderly Earl's large family of children, grandchildren, great-nephews and -nieces, that Lear made his first amusing drawings of odd-looking birds, animals, and people, with comic rhymes to accompany them. The delight with which they were received in the Earl of Derby's crowded nursery led to Lear's fame as a writer of curious verse. His *Book of Nonsense*, published in 1846, his rhymes known as 'limericks', and his comic alphabets became much better known than any of his fine pictures of birds.

Although Lear enjoyed his stay at Knowsley, he was worried that his eyesight was deteriorating and felt he needed rest from close, exacting work. Perhaps it was fear of eyestrain which made Lear create such large birds. Writing to Gould on October 31, 1836, he complained, 'My eyes are so sadly worse, that no bird under an ostrich shall I soon be able to do.'

In 1837 he decided to leave England and work abroad, painting landscape in a warmer climate, where he would feel fitter and stronger. By the following year, he had settled for the winter in Rome, the centre of a large colony of artists of many nationalities, and was able to tell Gould that he had found friends, pupils, and opportunities to paint so that he was 'over head and ears in employment. . . . You will lift up your hands and eyes and legs and possibly fall quite off your chair when I tell you I was enabled to send some of my earnings to my mother & sisters & to put by 100£ besides for the use of the summer.' He was anxious to assure Gould, who had advised him otherwise, that he was pleased he had taken up landscape, for in spite of his late start and inexperience, he was finding the work creative and challenging.

Lear, however, was not always happy in Rome. In a half-sad, half-jocular letter of February 27, 1841, to Gould, he confided how lonely he was: 'I wish to goodness I could get a wife! You have no idea how sick I am of living alone!! Please make a memorandum of any lady under 28 who has a little money—can live in Rome—and knows how to cut pencils and make puddings ... the wish of my life at present is quiet—to live in the country and paint landscapes—the cutting pencil pudding making lady included.'

Edward Lear never returned to England, except for occasional visits, or fully resumed his ornithological work. He spent an itinerant life, producing many illustrated travel books and landscapes of Italy, Greece, Egypt, and India. He finally settled, towards the end of his life, on the Italian Riviera at San Remo, with his famous striped cat 'Foss', his constant companion.

When Lear was told of Gould's death in 1881, he revealed that his memory of Gould was not an entirely pleasant one: 'He was one I never liked really, for, in spite of a certain jollity and bonhommie, he was a harsh and violent man. At the Zoological Society at 33 Bruton Street, at Hullmandels—at Broad Street ever the same, persevering hard working toiler in his own (ornithological) line,—but ever as unfeeling for those about him. In this earliest phase of his bird-drawing, he owed everything to his excellent wife, & to myself,—without whose help in drawing he had done nothing.' It is sad to learn that Lear did not have a happier recollection of Gould, although his surviving letters to Gould are friendly and jovial. Lear's temperament was sensitive, nervous, and prone to depression, so it is very probable that he must often have been at variance with the remorselessly energetic business-like ways of his employer.

## 13. THE BIRDS OF AUSTRALIA

For his next project John Gould tackled a completely new field, the birds of Australia. For some time he had been intrigued by the accounts and specimens of strange colourful birds which his wife's two brothers, Stephen and Charles Coxen who had emigrated to Australia, sent from this largely unexplored continent. Gould began the first two parts of the *Birds of Australia*, then abandoned the work, deciding he would have to go and find the exciting new material himself. It was a momentous decision, and Gould had to make many new plans and arrangements for himself and his family.

One of the manuscripts he had to leave unfinished was the text of the bird section of Charles Darwin's *Zoology of the Voyage of H.M.S. Beagle* (1832–36) which described the birds seen and collected on Darwin's famous voyage. It was from the field work carried out on this journey that Charles Darwin's theories of natural evolution slowly developed, to be eventually published in the controversial *Origin of Species* (1859). Darwin's writings met with censure and gave rise to bitter argument, but are now recognized, in the words of Julian Huxley, as 'the foundation for the entire structure of modern biology'.

The enterprise meant that Gould had to resign from his post at the Zoological Society. He had become Superintendant of the Ornithological Department of the Museum and had greatly increased their collections. He never resumed this work, for on his return he was too occupied with his books. Gould was made a Fellow in 1840 and served as Vice President for many years afterwards.

The financial side, the correspondence, and delivery and distribution of the books were left in the charge of Mr Edwin Prince, Gould's long-suffering and painstaking secretary. Gould had made about £7,000 from his books during the previous eight years, so he felt he could use all his savings for the trip which would take about two years.

The Goulds had also their growing family to consider. There were now four children, Henry seven and a half years old, Charles four, Eliza two, and Louisa only six months old. Mrs Gould was loathe to be parted from her young family, but it was decided to leave the three youngest children behind in the care of her mother, Mrs Coxen, and Mrs Mitchell, Mrs Coxen's niece.

The voyage naturally required much preparation. In a letter of 1838, Audubon wrote very scathingly about Gould's provisions and his ability as a field-worker: 'Mr. Gould the author of the Birds of Europe is about leaving this country for New Holland, or as it is now called Australia—He takes his Wife and Bairns with him, a Waggon the size of a Squatters Cabin and all such apparatus as will encumber him not a little—he has never travelled in the Woods, never salted his rump stakes with Gun Powder and how he will take to it, will be a "sin to Crockett".'

John and Elizabeth Gould set sail for Australia in May 1838, in the *Parsee* (348 tons), arriving at Hobart, Tasmania, after a four-month voyage. There were five others in the group: Henry Gould, their eldest son, aged seven and a half; Henry Coxen, a nephew, aged fifteen, who was to join his uncles; John Gilbert, a zoologist and Gould's assistant; and two servants. The voyage was a safe one, although the *Parsee* was wrecked shortly afterwards off south Australia, and Gould, restless as ever, was able to collect specimens of sea birds by being lowered into the sea in a boat.

In Tasmania, Gould, exploring inland and round the shore, was soon able to send home a large case of skins, skeletons, and eggs, while Elizabeth drew local plants and branches. They were made welcome and shown every kindness by the Governor and his wife, Sir John and Lady Franklin. Sir John Franklin later died tragically on his Arctic expedition, searching for the North-West Passage, 1847, and Lady Franklin spent twelve years sending relief parties to discover his fate. Elizabeth stayed at Government House during her husband's travels in South Australia and New South Wales. She remained there when her fifth child, Franklin, was born, named after the Governor and his wife. The baby was a 'fine, healthy, child', and, according to Elizabeth's letters home, he soon became 'a great pet with all the family'. Later, Lady Franklin, herself childless, wished to adopt him, but Elizabeth refused to part with 'her little Tasmanian'.

After eleven months in Tasmania, Elizabeth, the two children and two servants accompanied John Gould to Sydney, and then on to Newcastle, from where they at last travelled to Yarrundi, the farming property of the Coxen brothers, on the Dart Brook, a tributary of the Hunter River. The farm was prospering, for much wanted rain had appeared after a long drought. Gould travelled widely on horseback along the Liverpool Plains and into the interior for almost six months. Elizabeth wrote to her mother of the success of their work: 'The ornithology is highly interesting. Many of the birds possess very curious habits, which have not been publicly noticed. I think the great mass of information John has obtained cannot fail to render our work highly interesting to the scientific world.'

One of the 'very curious habits' that Gould observed was the building of strange sorts of tunnels or runways by pairs of bower birds. These structures, woven with twigs, were decorated with gay feathers, shells, bones, scraps of cloth, and other bright bric-a-brac. Gould sketched the satin bower birds, busy arranging their curious den, and puzzled over its purpose, commenting in a letter: 'This is certainly not the nest of the satin bird, but only a place of rendezvous for the bird.' Later, when a pair of bower birds arrived at the Zoo, it was realized that this building was indeed a sort of courtship pavilion where these birds could play and dance.

Another fascination for Gould were the budgerigars which 'flew to water holes in flocks up to one hundred strong'. Charles Coxen had successfully reared some birds and Gould brought two live budgerigars back to England, where it was realized that their 'extreme cheerfulness of disposition and sprightliness of manner' made them excellent cage birds. They have now become popular pets throughout the world.

Gould constantly exclaimed on the beauty of the many birds he saw—the radiant parrots, honeyeaters, magnificent lyre birds, and birds of paradise—but there was still much to be discovered, and John Gilbert remained behind travelling into West Australia. There he found hundreds of new species and supplied Gould with vital information. In 1845, Gilbert was tragically killed by aborigines in North Australia during an expedition with Ludwig Leichhardt.

When the Goulds returned to England in August 1840, they continued the *Birds of Australia*, their greatest pioneering work of research. In Australia, today, Gould's name is widely known, as it is associated with Australia's movement for preservation. Many children and adults belong to the *Gould League of Bird Lovers*, an organization formed to protect birds, many of which Gould first illustrated and named.

### 14. THE DEATH OF ELIZABETH GOULD

1841 was a tragic year for the Gould family. Elizabeth had been greatly relieved to find that her mother and the children had all kept well during her absence. 'I do hope I shall not be obliged ever again to leave them—it is too much,' she had written at the end of her stay in Australia. Unfortunately, their reunion was short-lived. Less than a year after their return to England, Elizabeth died, four days after the birth of her sixth child. She was thirty-seven years old.

The loss to John Gould was immeasurable, for as a partner it seemed she could never be replaced. He had depended on her industry, devotion and help in the early days of his publishing career and her artistic gifts had manifested themselves in hundreds of drawings and lithographs. Gould had warmly acknowledged her support in the introduction to the *Birds of Australia*. And now, without his illustrator's help, he felt that the difficulties of continuing his books were very great indeed.

### 15. H. C. RICHTER AND THE HUMMING-BIRDS

John Gould was fortunate to find, after some searching, another illustrator, Henry Constantine Richter, a young lithographer, who had contributed to G. R. Gray's *Genera of Birds*. H. C. Richter worked very well with Gould, collaborating with him for forty years and illustrating over a thousand plates. He was able to translate perfectly Gould's rough sketches into very competent and skilfully composed lithographs and his prints became the most familiar and best-loved of Gould plates.

Almost nothing was known of this artist until Christine E. Jackson published a carefully researched account of his life in 1978 in the *Journal of the Society of Bibliography: Natural History*. Born in about 1821 at Brompton, London, H. C. Richter came from an artistic family. His grandfather, John Augustus Richter, a German, had been an engraver, artist and scagliolist, making imitation marble columns for Greenwich Hospital and various large country houses. His father was also a noted painter and engraver and his sister exhibited miniature portraits at the Royal Academy, London.

Richter probably received artistic instruction at home, but does not appear to have used his talents other than in producing studies, drawings, and lithographs of birds. Perhaps he lacked creative imagination, or was swamped by his talented family or his employers, but he seemed content to remain a skilled draughtsman, translating the ideas of others into accomplished prints.

Richter's first work for Gould was to help complete the *Birds of Australia*, using Elizabeth's drawings. He then played a large part in the production of the *Monograph of the Humming-Birds*.

Gould had been greatly fascinated by these tiny birds from the American continent which have been called 'flying jewels'. His collection of mounted specimens accumulated to about 300 species and these were displayed in his house in Charlotte Street. His daughter, Eliza, described the gradual transformation of their home into a museum: 'The drawing room when first I remember it was very pretty with creamy walls and gold and rather pale blue curtains and

chair covers and a warm coloured all overish patterned carpet, but as father's collection of humming birds grew larger, and he mounted fresh cases for want of other room, they were collected there until it became almost too full to move about. The housemaid was not allowed in it with broom or duster except on rare occasions, so in time it looked anything but pretty and of course was not used as a drawing room.'

At the time of the Great Exhibition, 1851, when hundreds of people came to London from the provinces, Gould displayed his humming-birds in a temporary building in the Zoological Gardens, Regent's Park. Glass cases, mostly octagonal shaped, were specifically designed, and the light arranged with the help of canopies so that the iridescent colours on the bird's neck, head, or back could be seen to the best advantage. Queen Victoria noted in her diary, on June 10, 1851, that she and Prince Albert drove 'with our 3 girls, Alexandrina, & the 2 Ernests' to the Zoo to inspect 'a collection (in a room arranged specially for this purpose) of Gould's stuffed Humming Birds. It is the most beautiful and complete collection seen, & it is impossible to imagine anything so lovely as these little Humming Birds, their variety, & the extraordinary brilliance of their colours.' Gould charged sixpence admission for this exhibition which in 1851 saw 75,000 visitors. He also left a visitors' book, hoping to obtain names of possible subscribers to his books. A demonstration took place there, which showed how his colourists could capture the iridescence of these tiny birds' plumage by a special recipe of oil colour and varnish over gold leaf.

Gould himself saw his first humming-bird in Philadelphia, during a short visit to America with his son Charles, in 1857. It is probable that neither Richter or the colourists ever saw the real birds. The first live humming-bird arrived in London in 1904 and only lived fourteen days as it proved impossible to feed it its required diet of honey and insects.

## 16. WAS GOULD AN ARTIST?

A glimpse of Gould at work with his colleagues can be seen from Eliza Gould's reminiscences of her father: 'We saw very little of him all day, as he had early breakfast. ... Other times he was in his office at the back of the house, busy with his books and birds, in all of which Mr. Prince was his help, Mr. Richter and afterwards Mr. Hart alone did the lithographing or drawing from stone from father's sketches and colouring from the same. Of course the greater part of the colouring and all the printing was done away from the house and by others, but all the copy plates were done at home, and *every* thing was overlooked by father or Mr. Prince, and the latter had to make fair copies for the printing of father's writing. No light task sometimes as his hand was none of the clearest to make out.'

It is evident from this account that Gould directed every stage of the books' production, but his own artistic gifts and contribution have been difficult to gauge. Many contemporaries mention Gould's sketching ability, including Dr Bowdler Sharpe: 'He was always able to sketch, somewhat roughly perhaps, the positions in which the birds were to be drawn upon the plates, and no one could have a better "eye" for specific differences.' Many of these rough sketches survive, annotated with hastily scrawled instructions, such as 'Bird in front of plant', 'Legs green', 'the white stands out ... like ears'. Only very few bear his signature, as Gould would have thought this unnecessary.

Some drawings, such as the yellow-billed cuckoo in the Academy of Natural Sciences of Philadelphia, labelled: 'Sketched by Mr. John Gould of London at this Academy, May 1857', show a strong vigorous pencil line, as if Gould felt confident he could quickly show the vital characteristics of a bird. But it is not clear whether Gould could, or did, produce more finished or skilful work than these sketches and drawings. As there is no record of any artistic training, it seems most likely that he left the sophisticated and elaborate designing and colouring to the artists whom he employed.

An external view of the building at the Zoological Gardens, Regent's Park, which housed the exhibition of humming-birds collected by Gould. This engraving appeared in the *Illustrated London News*, June 12, 1852.

An engraving which portrays the dinner in the Iguanodon, organized in London by Sir Richard Owen, and which took place on New Year's Eve, 1853.

## 17. DINNER IN THE IGUANODON

The middle of the nineteenth century saw controversy over Charles Darwin's theories of evolution. One of the most uncompromising anti-Darwinians, Sir Richard Owen, had very particular ideas about prehistoric creatures. He inspired the artist and sculptor, Benjamin Waterhouse Hawkins, to make life-size models of extinct animals. These cement monsters were erected on islands in a lake in the grounds of the Crystal Palace, Sydenham, London, and were partially submerged daily so as to give the illusion of being inundated by a primeval tide. The work on the model of the iguanodon was long and arduous and to celebrate its near completion, Waterhouse Hawkins held a dinner party. He sent invitations, on pieces of the wing bone of a pterodactyl, to eminent naturalists, and John Gould was invited to be present on New Year's Eve, 1853, at four pm. Gould had known Hawkins as a lithographer, when he had illustrated the birds described by Gould in the *Zoology of the Voyage of H.M.S. Sulphur* (1843–1844).

The party of twenty-one guests took place *inside* the mould of the iguanodon, with Sir Richard Owen at the head of the table, placed appropriately in the head of the dinosaur. After a great many toasts, long speeches, and a sumptuous and elegantly served meal, Gould and the other guests returned to London by rail. They were no doubt bemused by Owen's dissertation on the megalosaurus, iguanodon, and dinornis, but impressed by the preparations for these huge models which can still be seen on the same site in the Crystal Palace grounds.

'The question may naturally suggest itself to some of my readers, what object I had in publishing a work on the Birds of Great Britain, when I had already completed a similar publication on the avifauna of Europe,' wrote Gould in the introduction to *Birds of Great Britain*, issued in five volumes with 367 plates (1862–73).

Although many of the same birds appeared in the *Birds of Europe*, thirty years earlier, Gould greatly enlarged the scope of illustration by including young birds, chicks, eggs, and nests. He described how not all chicks were blind, callow, and helpless, but some, like the grebe's, could clamber on their mother's back, or swim, almost immediately after bursting from their shells. Richter's lithograph shows these quaint day-old chicks, with their red- and blue-coloured faces and striped bodies, being given a ride by their mother. At the approach of danger, she could dive with them underneath the water. The moorhen's chicks too could, just after birth, thread their way amongst the floating leaves of the water-lily.

Gould was anxious to show the great variety of chicks' colouring, which varies from the moss-like marbling of the plovers to the red, hairy and fluffy faces of the coots, to the tortoise-shell blotches of the black-headed gull. An example of a very ugly baby bird is the stork's offspring, after a drawing and specimen which Gould obtained from Dr Kaup of Darmstadt, after a ten-year search.

Gould observed that while some birds like the nuthatch or the kingfisher showed little change of colour, other birds' plumage was continually altering before maturity. To demonstrate this, he illustrated young starlings, whose brown colours changed into spangled feathers, and a brown young rose-coloured pastor, which had not yet acquired the pinks and blacks of adulthood.

The young cuckoo presented an intriguing problem to Gould. Various naturalists had reported that three days after the cuckoo's egg had been hatched in the nest by its foster-parents, the other fledgelings had been found thrown out on to the ground. Gould felt that the young cuckoo, only three days old, was not strong enough to do this act himself, and it was the foster-parents, over-anxious to care for their large parasite fledgeling, who cleared out the nest and inadvertently caused the death of their own young. After he had published this text, Gould received a sketch and an account by a Mrs Hugh Blackburn, 'a lady of undoubted veracity and considerable ability', who had actually seen a young cuckoo, three or four days old, in the act of ejecting some meadow pipit fledgelings from their nest. Gould admitted his mistake and the scene was lithographed, to be inserted into the third volume. It showed the grisly sight of the Hercules-like baby cuckoo standing up and, with its embryonic arm-like wings, heaving the other less developed fledglings overboard.

Another additional plate was the charming picture of the ten long-tailed tits bunched together on a tulip tree branch. All are facing us except one, which kindly gives us a back view of its plumage. These tits could have flown from the elaborate nest, shown in the plate of the adult birds, which included moss, cow-hair, silvery lichen, and about two thousand feathers in its construction. Other nests, like the bullfinch's, were equally intricate; this one was placed on a platform made of numerous stalks of the wild plant, traveller's joy, and rested on a boxwood branch. The nest itself consisted of roots, tendrils, and hair formed into a perfect hemisphere. The house sparrow's nest was also a great feat of bird architecture, and Gould was so impressed by its beautiful construction that it was presented to the British Museum. House sparrows usually make smaller nests in the eaves of houses, but this large, dome-shaped structure was found in the branches of a tree.

As some birds live in very inaccessible places, their nests are difficult to obtain. Gould knew of some lesser spotted woodpeckers' nests in the lofty poplars of a friend's garden and persuaded their gardener, a Mr Briggs, 'at considerable risk to limb and body', to climb up and saw off some dead branches. They found that inside the round, cup-shaped holes made by the woodpecker, eggs had been laid amongst fine sawdust and wood chippings.

One of the delights of the *Birds of Great Britain* is the delicacy of the plants and branches, such as the pink flowering may, the larch, the gorse or the silver fir, which are arranged with the carefully placed birds to form perfectly balanced pictures. Richter's compositions, such as the three wrens on a hop branch, or the marsh warblers

A sketch showing two birds on a branch, drawn by Gould who signed it with only the initial 'G'.

balanced on the purple loosestrife, seem very simple, but are masterpieces of ingenious design. Sometimes the careful introduction of insects, butterflies, grubs, or even a spider, add a lively touch, for the birds seem to dart towards them to catch them for their young. The grouping of the small birds is wonderfully varied, and never dull, for the commonest birds with everyday plants are transformed into poetic vignettes. The blackbirds in the honeysuckle, the thrush guarding its nest in the dog-rose plant, the robin and its nestlings in the ivy, now favourite prints, are lyrical compositions with the most delicate details of plant and bird life.

Unexpectedly, the text accompanying the attractive plate of the goldfinch and the wild teasles, gives fascinating information on the interest in wild birds amongst the inhabitants of the London slums. Gould refers to the epic record of mid-Victorian social life, Henry Mayhew's *London Labour and the London Poor* (1851), which stated that about 200 persons gained a livelihood by capturing goldfinches, linnets, and other birds. Mayhew had a remarkable facility for capturing the actual rhythm of speech of the poor whose lives he recorded, including several street sellers of birds and birds' nests. One long talk was conducted with a young gypsy lad carrying 'in one hand his basket of nests, dotted with their many-coloured eggs' and in the other 'a live snake'. The lad states, 'I am a seller of birds'-nesties, snakes, hedgehogs, frogs, snails. ... The birds'-nesties from one penny to three pennies a-piece. ... Yes, I should say, I do sell about three hundred nests every year. ... There's one gentleman as I sells to is a wholesale dealer in window glass. He puts them into glass cases, and makes presents of them to his friends. I've sold him a hundred nesties, I'm sure.' Gould found that these sellers were 'excellent observers in their way' of the whereabouts of birds in the country round London and could report on the arrival of migrants from abroad.

Gould's special haunt for observing birds was on the banks of the river Thames, at Taplow, Clieveden, and Cookham. He would travel there, twenty-five miles from London, by train, spend many hours fishing, his only relaxation, and watching river life. As he was not far from Windsor, he felt 'the associations of boyhood ever flitting before me'. The *Birds of Great Britain* was Gould's last fully complete work and in many ways his happiest and most satisfying achievement.

The majority of the fine lithographs for the *Birds of Great Britain* was the meticulous work of H. C. Richter. A newcomer, William Hart, contributed about forty plates, but little is known of this artist. He stayed with Gould until 1881 and then helped Dr Bowdler Sharpe complete Gould's unfinished work. His colouring was richer than Richter's, and in the *Birds of Asia* he developed a more open, rounded style. These two lithographers made their own water-colours and designs from Gould sketches. About fifty-seven plates were adapted from Joseph Wolf's water-colours but, as this free-lance artist had a very individual relationship with Gould, his contribution to the books is described later.

The illustrations to the *Birds of Great Britain* were considered Gould's high watermark in publishing. Fifteen years later, Lord Lilford, preparing a similar work, wrote of Gould's books: 'For really beautiful and correct illustrations of British birds you will find Gould's great work on that subject in the Library, but the books are so large that you will require a boy to help you carry them from the house.' Although the prints are seen at their best in their original folio size, they are certainly heavy to handle. (An American librarian reckoned that the bound copies weigh about twenty pounds each). It is thus a great advantage to have them available in today's more convenient modern format.

## 19. JOSEPH WOLF

Of all the artists that illustrated Gould's work, Joseph Wolf was the most distinguished and knowledgeable. He contributed fifty-seven illustrations to the *Birds of Great Britain* and twenty-four to the *Birds of Asia*. Gould was keen to obtain Wolf's collaboration but Wolf, although a trained lithographer, was an independent character and preferred to paint subject pictures in oils and water-colours, rather than be committed to illustrating books.

Our knowledge of Joseph Wolf derives mainly from *The life of Joseph Wolf* by A. H. Palmer, son of the visionary painter, Samuel Palmer. This was published in 1895, when Wolf was seventy-five years old, and includes anecdotes about his friendship with Gould, usually told at Gould's expense. These mostly reveal that Wolf had an amused respect for the older man, but often felt that he was the better and more experienced naturalist.

Joseph Wolf, born in Germany in 1820, was sixteen years younger than Gould. He was brought up in the Rhineland, in a small village called Moerz, near Koblenz, at the confluence of the Rhine and the Moselle. His father farmed his own land and was looked upon as the head of the village community. Wolf's boyhood was spent roaming the beautiful Moselle valley; he enjoyed sketching birds out-of-doors and managed to capture and even tame birds of prey himself.

When Wolf was sixteen, he refused to follow the farming life of his father and was apprenticed to a firm of lithographers in Koblenz, where he designed labels and trade cards, including one, he related, for an 'Eagle Pharmacy'—his only opportunity to draw his favourite subject. But his interest was not in such routine work and he remained steadfast to his desire to portray birds and animals. He showed his water-colours of these to Dr Rüppell of Frankfurt, a subscriber to Gould's books who later employed Wolf for his *Birds of North-East Africa* and advised him to see Dr Kaup of Darmstadt Museum. The latter took his sketches to a conference in Leyden where Professor Schlegel saw them and commissioned Wolf to illustrate his treatise on falconry. The powerful water-colour of a magnificent hooded Greenland falcon resting on a falconer's gloved fist executed for Schlegel and Wulverhorst's *Traite de Fauconnerie* (1844–53) was later owned by John Gould. This book was inspired by the formation of a falconry club, at the Royal Castle of Loo in Holland, which raised falconry to the status it had had in the Middle Ages as a royal sport.

Wolf then decided to study oil-painting, first at Darmstadt and later at Antwerp Academy. His studies were interrupted when political unrest in Europe broke out in 1848, 'the year of revolutions'. He decided to accept an invitation from the elderly David Mitchell, then Secretary to the Zoological Society, to finish the illustrations of G. R. Gray's *Genera of Birds*. He arrived in London in February 1848 and soon started work at the British Museum.

Before long Wolf met John Gould, who already owned a small water-colour called *Partridges Dusting*, probably Wolf's first painting to be seen in England. Gould further commissioned an oil-painting, *Woodcocks Sheltering*, and this was shown at the Royal Academy Exhibition, in 1849, 'on the line', a coveted position on the wall at eye-level, at the request of the distinguished animal painter Sir Edwin Landseer. More opportunities arose, and the subject of woodcock nesting became a particular favourite, later occurring as a plate in Gould's *Birds of Great Britain*. Wolf had begun painting this subject as a youth, and Palmer describes how Wolf had discovered a covert and, 'with sketchbook in hand, and trembling all over with excitement, he crept up to the nest ... and worked "like blazes" till he had secured careful drawings from several points of view'.

Wolf's successful sketches were due to a detailed knowledge of feather formation, a special study he had made. He described the feather tracts of the woodcock: 'The light stripes on the backs of the birds of this genus are each composed of two lines of parti-coloured feathers; the light webs of which, joined together, form the stripes when the plumage is in perfect order. ... Professed ornithological artists have made the mistake of representing the stripe as formed of one line of feathers.'

Wolf was not completely satisfied with H. C. Richter's adaptation of his studies for the *Birds of Great Britain*. When he was looking at Gould's plates with A. H. Palmer, he exclaimed that the woodcock was '*much* too red, and he must go and put in those bluebells and things too! I can't be answerable for the colouring. Everything gets vulgarised.' Wolf preferred to use sombre colours and complained that Gould made his prints over-bright, justifying himself by saying, 'There are sure to be some specimens brighter than we do them.' An experiment of Wolf's, when living in London, was to place some mustard and cress he had grown with some partridges from a poulterer's shop and see how beautiful their sombre tones looked against the fresh green.

In the *Birds of Great Britain* there are three plates of another game

A pen and water-colour drawing of dotterels probably done by John Gould for the *Birds of Great Britain* (Collection Mrs A. Edelsten, London).

bird, the ptarmigan, in winter, summer, and autumn. Wolf enjoyed painting the camouflage of these birds' plumage, which was constantly changing, and one of his favourite subjects was the white ptarmigan crouching in the snow, while a golden eagle glides above unaware of its presence. Gould owned a water-colour of the winter ptarmigan; and another beautiful example of these soft, rounded, crouching white birds, with their blue-grey shadows, is in the Victoria and Albert Museum, London. Wolf made these studies in the Scottish Highlands and in Switzerland, where he enjoyed the solitude of the mountains. The plates also show how in summer the brown nesting females and chicks are camouflaged in the bracken—a contrast to the black cocks—and how in autumn their grey plumage is concealed amongst the misty mountains.

In 1856 Gould and Wolf went to Norway, where with gun, sketch-book, and skinning tools, they set off to study, amongst other subjects, the breeding habits of the fieldfares and the differences between Scottish and Norwegian willow grouse. In the bleak, wild moorland of Dovrefjell, with the Sneehatten mountains in the distance, Gould saw the golden plover, 'in the gayest dress with the young just hatched', and 'the Redwing, the Fieldfare, the Blue-throated Warbler, and a host of other birds breeding . . .' and he added, 'My visit to which will always be remembered with feelings of pleasure.' Wolf, on the other hand, described his stay less lyrically and later maintained to Palmer that he was the better field naturalist and could recognize bird song more easily. He related how the notes of the blue-throated warbler (also called the red-throated bluebreast) led him to find their hidden nest. Gould thought that this discovery was a chance one, and wrote, 'Mr. Wolf, who accompanied me to the celebrated Snee Hatten range of mountains, on the 1st of July, accidently discovered some young birds which were just forward enough to hop out of the nest—a great prize to me who had never before seen the bird at this age in a state of nature.' Gould gained a great deal of knowledge from this visit, but it is strange that the birds he studied there and then illustrated in the *Birds of Great Britain* (except for the golden plover) were executed not by Wolf, but by H. C. Richter.

The most powerful and magnificent of the Wolf illustrations were the birds of prey. Here again, can be seen his wonderful studies of plumage, for he could depict the precise, flecked and black and white markings of the Greenland falcon, the broad sweeping browns of the golden eagle, and the soft downy zig-zags of the snowy owl. In his conversations with Palmer, Wolf talked of the hard brittleness of a falcon's feather which falls to the ground unlike the soft fluffiness of an owl's feather which floats in the air.

Wolf also liked to show the grandeur and superiority of birds of prey. His oil-paintings bore titles such as *The Proud Bird of the Mountains, Jerfalcons attacking a Kite, Hunted Down*, revealing the struggle of strength and weakness. In Gould's plates, many birds of prey are shown with their victims—the little owl with a mouse, the buzzard with a hare, the osprey with a trout—thus portraying the predator's supremacy over lesser creatures. Gould greatly prized Wolf's birds of prey and owned an oil-painting of the Iceland falcon which stands majestically outlined against a snowy landscape.

The remaining illustrations by Wolf are mostly of ducks, gulls and waterfowl. The water-colours of the coot and the moorhen which Gould owned were painted in 1857, some years before the publication of the books. (Richter's alteration in this case was a more compact arrangement of the moorhen's chicks). From all evidence it seems, therefore, that Gould, unable to employ Wolf permanently as an illustrator, used the water-colours and oils he had in his possession. This may perhaps account for the distant pyramids and polar bears appearing in Wolf's backgrounds – hardly British scenes!

In Palmer's biography, Wolf gives a rather extraordinary account of how Gould acquired his studies, a yarn that perhaps became more colourful in the retelling. He describes how Gould kept a box of four-penny cigars, which Wolf especially liked, and had ready a number of sheets of drawing paper tacked on a board. When Wolf visited him, Gould would request a few sketches in a friendly way and persuade Wolf to do some life-size charcoal drawings which were later used for the *Birds of Great Britain*. On other occasions Gould would bring a newly acquired skin which he had 'borrowed' from a dealer, help himself to a cigar, and walk restlessly round the room while a sketch or sometimes a water-colour was being executed. 'Gould was a most restless fellow, who would never sit down except when he was fishing at Maidenhead when he would sit for hours.'

Although from Wolf's reminiscences it appears that there may have been a clash of personality between these two men, many ornithologists believe that Gould's finest plates were those produced by Joseph Wolf. Gould had enormous admiration for the German artist and frequently in his text was at great pains to praise and acknowledge Wolf's work.

The German ornithologist and illustrator Joseph Wolf by Lance Calkin (Zoological Society, London).

## 20. OLD AGE

From the middle of the 1870s, Gould's health was poor and he suffered from a painful disease. He still continued to work and plan books and, at his death in 1881, many publications were left unfinished. These included the *Birds of Asia*, his most protracted work, which he had started in 1850, and the *Birds of New Guinea*, containing some flamboyant birds of paradise, lithographed by William Hart. Dr Bowdler Sharpe assiduously completed these works and other unfinished texts.

Gould retained his enthusiasm for amassing skins and specimens until the end of his life. Dr Bowdler Sharpe has given us this description of Gould in old age: 'It was always a real pleasure to see the delight which animated the old naturalist when, in his invalid days, I took him some startling new form of bird such as Bulwer's Pheasant to be figured in the "Birds of Asia".'

An even more vivid account of Gould's addiction occurs in John Guille Millais' biography of his father. John Guille Millais was a bird and animal artist, the fourth son of the famous painter, Sir John Everett Millais, who, after early fame as a member of the Pre-Raphaelite Brotherhood, later became President of the Royal Academy. John Guille Millais visited Gould at Charlotte Street, with a friend who was a keen collector of birds-of-paradise skins and wished to purchase some rare specimens.

Millais records his impression of Gould, then in his seventies: 'He was at that time a confirmed invalid and confined to his couch, and when a drawer-full of birds was placed on his lap he would slowly and solemnly lift the lid and handle his specimens with fingers trembling with emotion.' After much persuasion and tact, Millais' friend was able to buy some much wanted skins at a high price. Much to Millais' surprise, Gould, who was then averse to strangers, asked to see his father, Sir John Everett Millais, and an appointment was made, probably in the last year of his life.

Gould sat propped up on his couch for the occasion, and calling his daughters to help him, showed his visitors 'his latest gems from New Guinea and the Papuan Islands, and afterwards his unique collection of humming-birds, all of which were set up in cases, and may now be seen (alas! with diminished lustre) in the Natural History Museum at South Kensington'.

Sir John Millais was delighted with all he saw, and on his way home said, 'That's a fine subject; a very fine subject. I shall paint it when I have time.' This resolution was carried out, for *The Ruling Passion* was exhibited at the Royal Academy in 1885. It showed an elderly ornithologist lying on his couch, scrutinizing a bird specimen, surrounded by his collection of stuffed creatures and his fascinated family. For the shrivelled old collector, Millais used an elderly engraver who, with skull-cap and spectacles, was quite unlike the photographs of Gould in old age. Millais' grandsons modelled for the children in the scene and the birds were supplied by his son. The painting is now in Glasgow Art Gallery, Scotland.

Unhappily, the scene in Millais' painting was not altogether true, for Gould was not surrounded by a large attentive family in old age. He never remarried and his three sons were absent, two by death and one abroad. In the introduction to the *Birds of Great Britain*, Gould mentions the loss of Franklin who had helped him prepare the book. They had travelled to Frencham Ponds, in Surrey, to find the Dartford warbler, and Franklin had sent him a white wagtail from San Remo, Italy. He died in 1873, aged thirty-three, on board ship in the Red Sea, during a voyage when he was in attendance to the Duke of Westminster's son, as a doctor. Henry Gould, also a doctor, had died in Bombay, in 1855, when he was only twenty-five. Charles Gould was a traveller and often supplied his father with information from far-off places, wandering through South America, China, Japan, and Tasmania. In 1886 he published a book called *Mythical Monsters* about legendary dragons and other creatures. He died in Montevideo, Uruguay, in 1893.

Gould's daughters, Eliza, Louisa, and Sai, lived sheltered lives, and, although accomplished in flower painting and sketching, were never allowed to help with their father's books. Eliza married in 1869 and had one daughter, the only grandchild.

In his old age, Gould must have wondered about the disposal of his treasured collection of skins. He offered his Australian material to the British Museum for £1,000, but this was refused, and they were sold instead to an American, Thomas B. Wilson, for the Academy of Natural Science, Philadelphia. The humming-birds and the remainder of his collection were sold after his death to the British Museum for £3,000.

Thirty tons of surplus book materials also survived Gould. These texts, drawings, proofs, tracings, and experimental prints were bought by the bookseller Henry Sotheran and remained, almost unexamined, in various basements and warehouses, wrapped in hundreds of parcels, until 1937, when they were sorted out and sold. Much of the stock reached America and was given to the University of Kansas by Ralph N. Ellis in 1945.

In his seventy-seven years, Gould had achieved a great deal: forty-one folio-sized volumes containing 2,999 hand-coloured lithographs. And he also published *The Monograph of the Kangaroos* (1841–44) and the *Mammals of Australia* (1845–63), both lively and exciting accounts of wild life in that unexplored continent. His scientific researches were widely acknowledged; he had been elected Fellow of the Royal Society, in 1843, when he was only thirty-nine years old.

Two years after Gould's death, Sir Richard Owen recalled the visits of his friend to his garden at Sheen Lodge, in Richmond Park. Owen was collecting for his 'garden book' the names of all the birds he could see: 'The list, however, would have been incomplete without the aid of my lamented friend, John Gould. It was ever with him a favourite summer afternoon's holiday, after a ramble in the park, to pass an hour in the garden. On one of these occasions, in early June, we rested on a seat by a weeping ash, but allowing a view of the lawn. Happening to show him my ornithological list at that date, Gould said, "You have got more birds in the garden than I see here, I expect." Now he possessed in a remarkable degree the faculty of imitating the various notes of all our vocal species. He bade us sit still and be silent, then began. After emitting a particular 'motivo' for a few minutes, he would quietly point to a little bird which had flown from an adjoining bush upon the lawn, and was there hopping to and fro, gradually nearing the locality of its specific song. We could then recognise the species to which Gould gave the name. This attraction and its result was repeated, and we enjoyed the same instructive amusement in subsequent summer vacations, to which I am indebted for additions that would otherwise probably have escaped my observation.'

This glimpse of John Gould is a fitting memorial to the celebrated ornithologist who liked simply to be called, 'John Gould: the Bird Man'.

*NOTE*
The subdivision of orders followed in this book – *Raptores, Insessores, Rasores, Grallatores, Natatores* – is the nineteenth-century one adopted by John Gould in his work, *Birds of Great Britain*. In the captions and the indices, however, we have followed present-day scientific classification:
– Common English name
– Scientific name (genus, species, sub-species)
– Name of the classifier
The name of the classifier is given without brackets when the species discovered and classified by him has kept its original name. It is put in brackets when the name has undergone changes by other classifiers.
"L" stands for Linnaeus.
– Subfamily (where relevant)
– Family
– Order

# Raptores

Birds of Prey and Owls

Egyptian Vulture

*Neophron percnopterus percnopterus* (L.)

Family *Accipitridae*

Order *Falconiformes*

Adult bird with young bird in the background.

1872

Golden Eagle

*Aquila chrysaëtos chrysaëtos* (L.)

Family *Accipitridae*

Order *Falconiformes*

Three or four-year-old adult bird (right) with prey (rabbit). In the background, nest with two young, and another adult bird in the vicinity.

1863

AQUILA NÆVIA.

HALIAÊTUS ALBICILLA.

Lesser Spotted Eagle

*Aquila pomarina pomarina* C.L.
  Brehm
Family *Accipitridae*
Order *Falconiformes*

Young bird with adult bird in the
background.
1870

White-tailed Eagle

*Haliaëtus albicilla* (Pallas)
Family *Accipitridae*
Order *Falconiformes*

Adult bird with adult bird in
flight near a colony of guillemots
in the background.
1863

Rough-legged Buzzard
*Buteo lagopus lagopus* (Pontoppidan)
Family *Accipitridae*
Order *Falconiformes*
Dark-phased adult bird with prey
(rabbit).
1864

Osprey
*Pandion haliaëtus haliaëtus* (L.)
Family *Pandionidae*
Order *Falconiformes*
Adult bird with prey (lake trout)
with another adult bird in the
background.
1870

ARCHIBUTEO LAGOPUS.

PANDION HALIAËTUS.

BUTEO VULGARIS.

Common Buzzard

*Buteo buteo buteo* (L.)
Family *Accipitridae*
Order *Falconiformes*

Adult birds in different phases of
coloration.
1863

PERNIS APIVORUS

Honey Buzzard

*Pernis apivorus* (L.)
Family *Accipitridae*
Order *Falconiformes*

A male feeds off a wasps' nest.
Behind him, the female with two
of her young.
1866

ASTUR PALUMBARIUS.

ACCIPITER NISIS.

Goshawk
*Accipiter gentilis gentilis* (L.)
Family *Accipitridae*
Order *Falconiformes*
Female (right) with young bird.
1869

Sparrowhawk
*Accipiter nisus nisus* (L.)
Family *Accipitridae*
Order *Falconiformes*
Male (right) with female preying
on a House Sparrow.
1864

Icelandic Gyrfalcon (opposite)
*Falco rusticolus islandicus* (L.)
Family *Falconidae*
Order *Falconiformes*
Adult bird, in the background
with prey.
1872

FALCO CANDICANS, *J.E.Gmel.*

Greenland Falcon, light race, adult and young.

Walter Imp.

FALCO CANDICANS.

Greenland Falcon, dark race, adult.

Walter Imp.

Greenland Gyrfalcon

*Falco rusticolus candicans* (L.)
Family *Falconidae*
Order *Falconiformes*

Adult bird (right) with young
with unusually light plumage.
1873

Greenland Gyrfalcon

*Falco rusticolus candicans* (L.)
Family *Falconidae*
Order *Falconiformes*

Dark-phased adult birds; on the
left, with prey (Mallard).
1873

FALCO CANDICANS.

Greenland Falcon, dark race young.

J.W.& & H.C. Richter del et lith.

Waller, Imp.

FALCO GYRFALCO, Linn.

Norwegian Falcon, adult and young.

J.W.& & H.C. Richter del et lith.

Waller Imp.

Greenland Gyrfalcon

*Falco rusticolus candicans* (L.)
Family *Falconidae*
Order *Falconiformes*

Dark-phased young bird with
prey (partridge), and an adult bird
in flight in the background.
1873

Gyrfalcon

*Falco rusticolus rusticolus* L.
Family *Falconidae*
Order *Falconiformes*

Adult bird with crouching young.
1872

FALCO SUBBUTEO, Linn.

Hobby
*Falco subbuteo subbuteo* L.
Family *Falconidae*
Order *Falconiformes*

Male with dragonfly in its claws.
1865

FALCO PEREGRINUS, Gmel

Peregrine Falcon
*Falco peregrinus peregrinus* Tunstall
Family *Falconidae*
Order *Falconiformes*

Female, with an adult preying on
a male Mallard in flight in the
background.
1862

FALCO ISLANDUS, *J.F.Gmel.*

Iceland Falcon young.

Icelandic Gyrfalcon
*Falco rusticolus islandicus* (L.)
Family *Falconidae*
Order *Falconiformes*
Young bird.
1872

FALCO ÆSALON, *Linn.*

Merlin
*Falco columbarius aesalon* Tunstall
Family *Falconidae*
Order *Falconiformes*
Adult birds in the nest; male with wings spread open holding prey (Serin) for the young, below the female.
1865

ERYTHROPUS VESPERTINUS.

Red-footed Falcon
*Falco vespertinus vespertinus* L.
Family *Falconidae*
Order *Falconiformes*
Male (above left) with female.
1869

TINNUNCULUS ALAUDARIUS.

Kestrel
*Falco tinnunculus tinnunculus* L.
Family *Falconidae*
Order *Falconiformes*
Male (foreground) with female
and another male in flight.
1862

MILVUS REGALIS.

MILVUS MIGRANS, Bodd.

Red Kite

*Milvus milvus milvus* (L.)
Family *Accipitridae*
Order *Falconiformes*

Males, with nest in the
background.
1868

Black Kite

*Milvus migrans migrans* (Boddaert)
Family *Accipitridae*
Order *Falconiformes*

Adult bird.
1872

CIRCUS ÆRUGINOSUS.

Marsh Harrier

*Circus aeruginosus aeruginosus* (L.)
Family *Accipitridae*
Order *Falconiformes*

Male, with young bird squatting
behind.
1868

Marsh Harrier

*Circus aeruginosus aeruginosus* (L.)
Family *Accipitridae*
Order *Falconiformes*

Adult females fight over a snake.
1868

CIRCUS ÆRUGINOSUS.

CIRCUS CYANEUS.

Hen Harrier

*Circus cyaneus cyaneus* (L.)
Family *Accipitridae*
Order *Falconiformes*

Male, with female in flight.
1867

Montagu's Harrier

*Circus pygargus* (L.)
Family *Accipitridae*
Order *Falconiformes*

Male feeding off a mole, with female behind.
1867

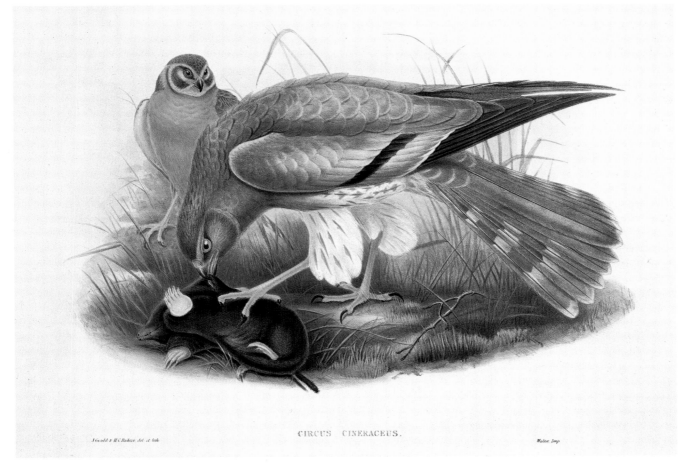

CIRCUS CINERACEUS.

STRIX FLAMMEA, Linn

SYRNIUM ALUCO.

Barn Owl

*Tyto alba alba* (Scopoli)
Subfamily *Tytoninae*
Family *Strigidae*
Order *Strigiformes*

Adult birds with young in the
nest-cavity.
1869

Tawny Owl

*Strix aluco aluco* L.
Subfamily *Striginae*
Family *Strigidae*
Order *Strigiformes*

Adult birds with young in the
nest-cavity.
1864

Eagle Owl (opposite)

*Bubo bubo bubo* (L.)
Subfamily *Striginae*
Family *Strigidae*
Order *Strigiformes*

Adult bird offering a rabbit to its
young in the nest.
1866

Long-eared Owl

*Asio otus otus* (L.)
Subfamily *Striginae*
Family *Strigidae*
Order *Strigiformes*

Adult birds with their young
in the nest.
1863

OTUS VULGARIS.

Short-eared Owl

*Asio flammeus flammeus*
 (Pontoppidan)
Subfamily *Striginae*
Family *Strigidae*
Order *Strigiformes*

Adult bird in the nest with
eggs, with adult bird in flight.
1863

BRACHYOTUS PALUSTRIS.

SCOPS ZORCA.

NYCTEA NIVEA.

Scops Owl

*Otus scops scops* (L.)
Subfamily *Striginae*
Family *Strigidae*
Order *Strigiformes*

Dark- and grey-phased adult
birds, with a Death's Head Hawk
Moth in its beak (left).
1868

Snowy Owl

*Nyctea scandiaca* (L.)
Subfamily *Striginae*
Family *Strigidae*
Order *Strigiformes*

Female (foreground) with light-
and dark-phased adult birds.
1863

SURNIA FUNEREA.

NYCTALE TENGMALMI.

Hawk Owl
*Surnia ulula* (L.)
Subfamily *Striginae*
Family *Strigidae*
Order *Strigiformes*
Adult birds.
1867

Tengmalm's Owl
*Aegolius funereus funereus* (L.)
Subfamily *Striginae*
Family *Strigidae*
Order *Strigiformes*
Adult bird with prey in its beak.
1867

ATHENE NOCTUA.

Little Owl

*Athene noctua noctua* (Scopoli)
Subfamily *Striginae*
Family *Strigidae*
Order *Strigiformes*

Adult bird in the nest-cavity with
its young and prey.
1867

# *Insessores*

## Nightjars, Swifts, Kingfishers and their Allies, and Perching Birds

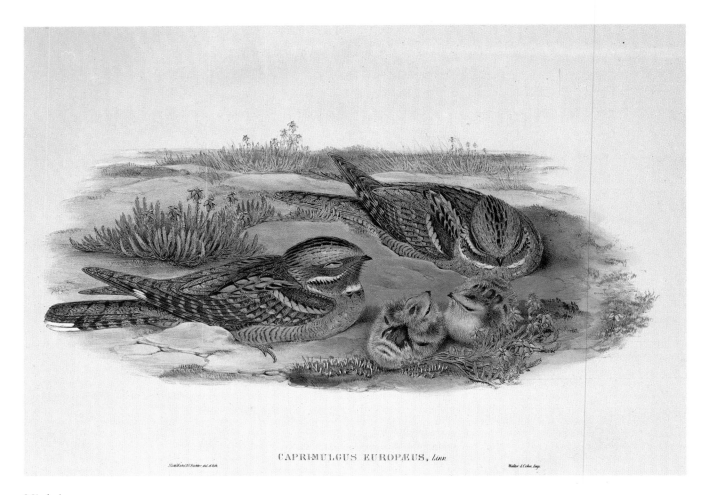

CAPRIMULGUS EUROPÆUS, *Linn*

Nightjar
*Caprimulgus europaeus europaeus* L.
Family *Caprimulgidae*
Order *Caprimulgiformes*
Adults with their young.
1863

Red-necked Nightjar
*Caprimulgus ruficollis ruficollis*
Temminck
Family *Caprimulgidae*
Order *Caprimulgiformes*
Male (right) with female.
1871

CAPRIMULGUS RUFICOLLIS, *Temm*

CYPSELUS APUS.

Swift

*Apus apus apus* (L.)
Subfamily *Apodinae*
Family *Apodidae*
Order *Apodiformes*

Adult bird feeds its young in the nest.
1862

CYPSELUS MELBA.

Alpine Swift

*Apus melba melba* (L.)
Subfamily *Apodinae*
Family *Apodidae*
Order *Apodiformes*

Adult birds.
1869

HIRUNDO RUSTICA, *Linn.*

CHELIDON URBICA.

Barn Swallow
*Hirundo rustica rustica* L.
Family *Hirundinidae*
Order *Passeriformes*

Adult bird feeding young bird in flight.
1863

House Martin
*Delichon urbica urbica* (L.)
Family *Hirundinidae*
Order *Passeriformes*

Adult birds playing in flight.
1869

Sand Martin

*Riparia riparia riparia* (L.)
Family *Hirundinidae*
Order *Passeriformes*

Adult bird in flight, with nest-
building colony in the
background.
1863

COTYLE RIPARIA.

Sand Martin

*Riparia riparia riparia* (L.)
Family *Hirundinidae*
Order *Passeriformes*

Young bird, with flocks in the
background gathering together
to migrate.
1873

COTYLE RIPARIA.

MEROPS APIASTER. *Linn*.

Bee-eater

*Merops apiaster* L.
Family *Meropidae*
Order *Coraciformes*

Male (left) with young bird.
1867

ALCEDO ISPIDA, *Linn*.

Kingfisher

*Alcedo atthis ispida* L.
Family *Alcedinidae*
Order *Coraciformes*

Adult birds.
1864

CORACIAS GARRULA, *Linn.*

UPUPA EPOPS, *Linn.*

Blue Roller

*Coracias garrulus garrulus* L.
Subfamily *Coraciinae*
Family *Coraciidae*
Order *Coraciiformes*

Male (foreground) with female.
1866

Hoopoe

*Upupa epops epops* L.
Subfamily *Upupinae*
Family *Upupidae*
Order *Coraciiformes*

Adult birds feeding their young
in the nest-cavity.
1868

LANIUS EXCUBITOR, *Linn*

LANIUS MINOR, *Gmel*

Great Grey Shrike
*Lanius excubitor excubitor* L.
Family *Laniidae*
Order *Passeriformes*
Male adding a shrew mouse to its
food reserve.
1868

Lesser Grey Shrike
*Lanius minor minor* Gmelin
Family *Laniidae*
Order *Passeriformes*
Adult birds.
1868

ENNEOCTONUS RUFUS.

Red-backed Shrike
*Lanius collurio collurio* L.
Family *Laniidae*
Order *Passeriformes*
Male (above) with female by the
food reserve.
1862

Woodchat Shrike
*Lanius senator senator* L.
Family *Laniidae*
Order *Passeriformes*
Adult birds.
1862

ENNEOCTONUS COLLURIO

MUSCICAPA ATRICAPILLA, *Linn.*

MUSCICAPA COLLARIS, *Bechst.*

Pied Flycatcher
*Ficedula hypoleuca hypoleuca* (Pallas)
Subfamily *Muscicapinae*
Family *Muscicapidae*
Order *Passeriformes*

Male (above) with female (below
left) and young bird (below
right).
1863

White-collared Flycatcher
*Ficedula albicollis albicollis*
 (Temminck)
Subfamily *Muscicapinae*
Family *Muscicapidae*
Order *Passeriformes*

Male (left) with young female.
1873

BUTALIS GRISOLA.

ERYTHROSTERNA PARVA.

Spotted Flycatcher

*Muscicapa striata striata* (Pallas)
Subfamily *Muscicapinae*
Family *Muscicapidae*
Order *Passeriformes*

Male.
1863

Red-breasted Flycatcher

*Ficedula parva parva* (Bechstein)
Subfamily *Muscicapinae*
Family *Muscicapidae*
Order *Passeriformes*

Male (above) with female.
1869

AMPELIS GARRULUS.

Bohemian Waxwing

*Bombycilla garrulus garrulus*
Subfamily *Bombycillinae*
Family *Bombycillidae*
Order *Passeriformes*

Adult birds in the nest with their young.
1867

SITTA CÆSIA, *Wolf et Meyer*

Nuthatch

*Sitta europaea europaea* Sachtleben
Subfamily *Sittinae*
Family *Sittidae*
Order *Passeriformes*

Adult birds by the nest-cavity.
1863

**PARUS MAJOR.** *Linn.*

Great Tit
*Parus major major* L.
Family *Paridae*
Order *Passeriformes*
Adult birds.
1867

**PARUS CÆRULEUS.**

Blue Tit
*Parus cæruleus cæruleus* L.
Family *Paridae*
Order *Passeriformes*
Adult birds.
1862

PARUS ATER.

PARUS CRISTATUS, Linn

Coal Tit
*Parus ater ater* L.
Family *Paridae*
Order *Passeriformes*
Adult birds.
1862

Crested Tit
*Parus cristatus cristatus* L.
Family *Paridae*
Order *Passeriformes*
Adult birds.
1867

POECILE PALUSTRIS.

J. Gould & H C Richter, del. et lith.

Walter, Imp.

Marsh Tit

*Parus palustris palustris* L.
Family *Paridae*
Order *Passeriformes*

Adult birds.
1866

MECISTURA CAUDATA.

J. Gould and H C Richter del et lith.

Walter & Cohn, Imp.

Long-tailed Tit

*Aegithalos caudatus europaeus*
 (Hermann)
Family *Aegithalidae*
Order *Passeriformes*

Adult birds feed their young in
the nest.
1862

MECISTURA CAUDATA.
Young.

CALAMOPHILUS BIARMICUS.

Long-tailed Tit

*Aegithalos caudatus europaeus*
 (Hermann)
Family *Aegithalidae*
Order *Passeriformes*

Young birds who have newly left
the nest.
1873

Bearded Tit

*Panurus biarmicus biarmicus* (L.)
Subfamily *Panurinae*
Family *Timaliidae*
Order *Passeriformes*

Male (above) with female, below
nest with young.
1862

Golden Oriole (opposite)

*Oriolus oriolus oriolus* (L.)
Family *Oriolidae*
Order *Passeriformes*

Male (above) with female sitting
on eggs.
1865

Song Thrush
*Turdus philomelos philomelos* C.L.
  Brehm
Family *Turdidae*
Order *Passeriformes*
Male by the nest with eggs and
above, female singing.
1866

Mistle Thrush
*Turdus viscivorus viscivorus* L.
Family *Turdidae*
Order *Passeriformes*
Adult bird with young below.
1869

TURDUS ILIACUS, *Linn.*

TURDUS PILARIS, *Linn.*

Fieldfare
*Turdus pilaris* L.
Family *Turdidae*
Order *Passeriformes*

Male (below) with female in the
nest sitting on eggs.
1864

Redwing
*Turdus iliacus iliacus* L.
Family *Turdidae*
Order *Passeriformes*

Male, about to fly, feeds on
buckthorn berries.
1864

TURDUS ATROGULARIS, *Temm.*

MERULA VULGARIS, *Ray.*

Black-throated Thrush
*Turdus ruficollis atrogularis*
 Jarocki
Family *Turdidae*
Order *Passeriformes*
Male singing (above) with female.
1871

Blackbird
*Turdus merula merula* L.
Family *Turdidae*
Order *Passeriformes*
Male with female sitting on eggs
in the nest.
1866

MERULA TORQUATA.

OREOCINCLA AUREA.

Ring Ouzel

*Turdus torquatus torquatus* L.
Family *Turdidae*
Order *Passeriformes*

Male (right) with female feeding
her young in the nest.
1867

Golden Thrush

*Zoothera dauma aurea* (Holandre)
Family *Turdidae*
Order *Passeriformes*

Adult bird.
1869

CICHLOSELYS SIBIRICUS.

Siberian Thrush
*Turdus sibiricus sibiricus* Pallas
Family *Turdidae*
Order *Passeriformes*
Male (left) with female.
1873

Dipper
*Cinclus cinclus cinclus* (L.)
Family *Cinclidae*
Order *Passeriformes*
Adult bird of the Central-
European species feeding its
young in the nest.
1862

CINCLUS AQUATICUS.

CINCLUS MELANOGASTER, Brehm.

J.Gould & H.C.Richter del et lith.                                    Walter Imp.

Black-bellied Water Ouzel
*Cinclus cinclus aquaticus*
 Bechstein
Family *Cinclidae*
Order *Passeriformes*
Adult birds of the North-
European species.
1871

PETROCOSSYPHUS CYANUS.

J.Gould & H.C.Richter del et lith.                                    Walter Imp.

Blue Rock Thrush
*Monticola solitarius solitarius* (L.)
Family *Turdidae*
Order *Passeriformes*
Male (right) with female.
1872

PETROCINCLA SAXATILIS.

Rock Thrush
*Monticola saxatilis* (L.)
Family *Turdidae*
Order *Passeriformes*
Male singing by the nest, with female.
1869

SAXICOLA ŒNANTHE.

Wheatear
*Oenanthe oenanthe oenanthe* (L.)
Family *Turdidae*
Order *Passeriformes*
Male (foreground) with female.
1868

PRATINCOLA RUBETRA.

PRATINCOLA RUBICOLA.

Whinchat
*Saxicola rubetra* (L.)
Family *Turdidae*
Order *Passeriformes*

Male (foreground) with female.
1864

Stonechat
*Saxicola torquata rubicola* (L.)
Family *Turdidae*
Order *Passeriformes*

Male (above) with female.
1864

Red-throated Bluebreast
*Luscinia svecica svecica* (L.)
Family *Turdidae*
Order *Passeriformes*
Male (right) with female.
1865

Robin
*Erithacus rubecula rubecula* (L.)
Family *Turdidae*
Order *Passeriformes*
Adult birds feeding their young
in the nest.
1866

White-throated Bluebreast
*Luscinia svecica cyanecula* (Meisner)
Family *Turdidae*
Order *Passeriformes*
Male (right), with female feeding
her young in the nest.
1873

Redstart
*Phoenicurus phoenicurus phoenicurus*
 (L.)
Family *Turdidae*
Order *Passeriformes*
Female in the nest-cavity, with
two males.
1864

RUTICILLA TITHYS.

AEDON GALACTODES.

Black Redstart
*Phoenicurus ochruros gibraltariensis*
  (Gmelin)
Family *Turdidae*
Order *Passeriformes*

Male (centre) with female and
nest with eggs.
1864

Rufous Warbler
*Cercotrichas galactotes galactotes*
  (Temminck)
Family *Turdidae*
Order *Passeriformes*

Adult birds.
1870

ACCENTOR ALPINUS.

ACCENTOR MODULARIS.

Alpine Accentor
*Prunella collaris collaris* (Scopoli)
Family *Prunellidae*
Order *Passeriformes*

Male (right) with female.
1868

Dunnock
*Prunella modularis modularis* (L.)
Family *Prunellidae*
Order *Passeriformes*

Male (below) with female.
1868

Nightingale
*Luscinia megarhynchos megarhynchos*
C.L. Brehm
Family *Turdidae*
Order *Passeriformes*

Male (left) with female sitting on eggs.
1867

Whitethroat
*Sylvia communis communis* Lathan
Subfamily *Sylviinae*
Family *Sylviidae*
Order *Passeriformes*

Adult birds.
1865

Dartford Warbler (opposite)
*Sylvia undata undata* (Boddaert)
Subfamily *Sylviinae*
Family *Sylviidae*
Order *Passeriformes*

Male (above) with female.
1862

84

85

Lesser Whitethroat
*Sylvia curruca curruca* (L.)
Subfamily *Sylviinae*
Family *Sylviidae*
Order *Passeriformes*
Female (left) with male.
1865

Blackcap
*Sylvia atricapilla atricapilla* (L.)
Subfamily *Sylviinae*
Family *Sylviidae*
Order *Passeriformes*
Male (above) with female.
1865

CURRUCA ORPHEA.

CURRUCA HORTENSIS.

Orphean Warbler

*Sylvia hortensis hortensis* (Gmelin)
Subfamily *Sylviinae*
Family *Sylviidae*
Order *Passeriformes*

Male (above) with female.
1872

Garden Warbler

*Sylvia borin borin* (Boddaert)
Subfamily *Sylviinae*
Family *Sylviidae*
Order *Passeriformes*

Female (above) with male.
1865

TROGLODYTES EUROPÆUS.

Treecreeper
*Certhia familiaris macrodactyla* C.L.
 Brehm
Family *Certhiidae*
Order *Passeriformes*

Male (below) with female feeding
her young in the nest.
1868

CERTHIA FAMILIARIS, *Linn.*

Wren
*Troglodytes troglodytes troglodytes* (L.)
Family *Troglodytidae*
Order *Passeriformes*

Adult birds feeding young bird.
1863

PHYLLOPNEUSTE TROCHILUS.

Willow Warbler
*Phylloscopus trochilus trochilus* (L.)
Subfamily *Sylviinae*
Family *Sylviidae*
Order *Passeriformes*
Male (left) with female.
1862

PHYLLOPNEUSTE RUFA.

Chiffchaff
*Phylloscopus collybita collybita*
 (Vieillot)
Subfamily *Sylviinae*
Family *Sylviidae*
Order *Passeriformes*
Male (above) with female.
1862

89

PHYLLOPNEUSTE SIBILATRIX.

Wood Warbler
*Phylloscopus sibilatrix* (Bechstein)
Subfamily *Sylviinae*
Family *Sylviidae*
Order *Passeriformes*
Male (below) with female.
1962

REGULOIDES SUPERCILIOSUS.

Yellow-browed Warbler
*Phylloscopus inornatus inornatus*
 (Blyth)
Subfamily *Sylviinae*
Family *Sylviidae*
Order *Passeriformes*
Adult birds.
1869

REGULUS CRISTATUS, *Ray*

REGULUS IGNICAPILLUS.

Goldcrest

*Regulus regulus regulus* (L.)
Subfamily *Regulinae*
Family *Sylviidae*
Order *Passeriformes*

Female (below) with males.
1863

Firecrest

*Regulus ignicapillus ignicapillus*
  (Temminck)
Subfamily *Regulinae*
Family *Sylviidae*
Order *Passeriformes*

Males (above) with female.
1863

FICEDULA HYPOLAIS.

ACROCEPHALUS TURDOÏDES.

Melodius Warbler
*Hippolais polyglotta* (Vieillot)
Subfamily *Sylviinae*
Family *Sylviidae*
Order *Passeriformes*

Adult bird singing.
1865

Great Reed Warbler
*Acrocephalus arundinaceus
  arundinaceus* (L.)
Subfamily *Sylviinae*
Family *Sylviidae*
Order *Passeriformes*

Adult bird.
1870

Reed Warbler

*Acrocephalus scirpaceus scirpaceus*
(Hermann)
Subfamily *Sylviinae*
Family *Sylviidae*
Order *Passeriformes*

Adult birds.
1862

CALAMOHERPE PALUSTRIS.

Marsh Warbler

*Acrocephalus palustris* (Bechstein)
Subfamily *Sylviinae*
Family *Sylviidae*
Order *Passeriformes*

Female (below) with male.
1872

CALAMOHERPE ARUNDINACEA.

CALAMODYTA PHRAGMITIS.

CALAMODYTA AQUATICA.

Aquatic Warbler
*Acrocephalus paludicola* (Vieillot)
Subfamily *Sylviinae*
Family *Sylviidae*
Order *Passeriformes*
Adult birds.
1862.

Sedge Warbler
*Acrocephalus schoenobaenus* (L.)
Subfamily *Sylviinae*
Family *Sylviidae*
Order *Passeriformes*
Female (below) with male.
1871

Savi's Warbler
*Locustella luscinioides luscinioides*
 (Savi)
Subfamily *Sylviinae*
Family *Sylviidae*
Order *Passeriformes*

Male (above) with female sitting on eggs in nest. 1866

LUSCINIOPSIS LUSCINIOIDES.

J. Gould & H. C. Richter del. et lith.                    Walter Imp.

Grasshopper Warbler
*Locustella naevia naevia*
 (Boddaert)
Subfamily *Sylviinae*
Family *Sylviidae*
Order *Passeriformes*

Male (left) with female. 1866

LOCUSTELLA AVICULA, *Ray*

J. Gould & H. C. Richter del. et lith.                    Walter Imp.

# Insessores

Perching Birds, Cuckoos, and Woodpeckers

MOTACILLA YARRELLI.

J. Gould & H.C. Richter, del. et lith.    Walter, Imp.

Pied Wagtail
*Motacilla alba yarrelli* Gould
Family *Motacillidae*
Order *Passeriformes*

Male (right) with young bird
(centre) and female.
1867

White Wagtail
*Motacilla alba alba* L.
Family *Motacillidae*
Order *Passeriformes*

Male and female in summer
plumage.
1867

MOTACILLA ALBA, *Linn.*

J. Gould & H.C. Richter, del. et lith.    Walter, Imp.

BUDYTES RAYI.

Yellow Wagtail
*Motacilla flava flavissima* (Blyth)
Family *Motacillidae*
Order *Passeriformes*
Female (right) with male.
1868

Grey-headed Wagtail
*Motacilla flava flava* L.
Family *Motacillidae*
Order *Passeriformes*
Female (centre) with males.
1868

BUDYTES FLAVA.

Spanish Wagtail
*Motacilla flava iberiae*
Hartet
Male (right) with
female (centre).

Grey-capped Wagtail
*Motacilla flava
cinereocapilla* Savi
Family *Motacillidae*
Order *Passeriformes*
Left, male.
1872

BUDYTES CINEREOCAPILLA.

Grey Wagtail
*Motacilla cinerea cinerea*
Tunstall
Family *Motacillidae*
Order *Passeriformes*

Adult birds in summer
plumage (centre and
right) with young
birds.
1868

CALOBATES SULPHUREA.
Summer plumage.

Grey Wagtail
*Motacilla cinerea cinerea*
 Tunstall
Family *Motacillidae*
Order *Passeriformes*
Adult birds in autumn, already
in their winter plumage.
1868

CALOBATES SULPHUREA.

Richard's Pipit
*Anthus novaeseelandiae richardi*
 Vieillot
Family *Motacillidae*
Order *Passeriformes*
Males in their winter plumage.
1867

ANTHUS RICHARDI.

ANTHUS CAMPESTRIS. *Bechst*

Tawny Pipit

*Anthus campestris campestris* (L.)
Family *Motacillidae*
Order *Passeriformes*

Male (left) with female.
1866

ANTHUS OBSCURUS.

Rock Pipit

*Anthus spinoletta littoralis* C.L.
 Brehm
Family *Motacillidae*
Order *Passeriformes*

Bird in nuptial plumage (right)
with bird in non-breeding
plumage.
1867

ANTHUS SPINOLETTA.

Water Pipit
*Anthus spinoletta spinoletta* (L.)
Family *Motacillidae*
Order *Passeriformes*
Bird in nuptial plumage (right)
with bird in non-breeding
plumage.
1867

ANTHUS CERVINUS.

Red-throated Pipit
*Anthus cervinus* (Pallas)
Family *Motacillidae*
Order *Passeriformes*
Bird in nuptial plumage (right)
with bird in non-breeding
plumage.
1873

ALAUDA ARVENSIS. *Linn*

ALAUDA ARBOREA. *Linn*

Sky Lark
*Alauda arvensis arvensis* L.
Family *Alaudidae*
Order *Passeriformes*
Adult bird feeding its young in
the nest.
1869

Wood Lark
*Lullula arborea arborea* (L.)
Family *Alaudidae*
Order *Passeriformes*
Adult birds.
1869

ANTHUS PRATENSIS.

Meadow Pipit

*Anthus pratensis pratensis* (L.)
Family *Motacillidae*
Order *Passeriformes*.

Adult birds.
1863

ANTHUS ARBOREUS, *Bechst.*

Tree Pipit

*Anthus trivialis trivialis* (L.)
Family *Motacillidae*
Order *Passeriformes*

Adult birds.
1866

GALERITA CRISTATA, Bote

Crested Lark
*Galerida cristata cristata* (L.)
Family *Alaudidae*
Order *Passeriformes*
Male (right) with female.
1866

OTOCORIS ALPESTRIS.

Horned Lark
*Eremophila alpestris flava*
  (Gmelin)
Family *Alaudidae*
Order *Passeriformes*
Male (right) with young birds
(centre) and female.
1870

MELANOCORYPHA CALANDRA.

MELANOCORYPHA LEUCOPTERA.

Calandra Lark
*Melanocorypha calandra calandra* (L.)
Family *Alaudidae*
Order *Passeriformes*
Male (right) with female.
1872

White-winged Lark
*Melanocorypha leucoptera* (Pallas)
Family *Alaudidae*
Order *Passeriformes*
Male (right) with female.
1871

CALANDRELLA BRACHYDACTYLA.

Short-toed Lark
*Calandrella cinerea brachydactyla*
 (Leisler)
Family *Alaudidae*
Order *Passeriformes*
Adult (left) with young bird.
1869

EMBERIZA CITRINELLA. Linn.

Yellow Bunting
*Emberiza citrinella citrinella* L.
Family *Emberizidae*
Order *Passeriformes*
Male (above) with female.
1866

108

Cirl Bunting
*Emberiza cirlus cirlus* L.
Family *Emberizidae*
Order *Passeriformes*
Male (left) with female.
1866

EMBERIZA RUSTICA: *Pall.*

Jikenid & H.C.Richter del et lith.     Walter Imp.

Rustic Bunting
*Emberiza rustica rustica* Pallas
Family *Emberizidae*
Order *Passeriformes*
Male (below) with female.
1871

EMBERIZA CIRLUS, *Linn.*

J. Gould & H.C.Richter del. et lith.     Walter Imp.

EMBERIZA PUSILLA, *Pall.*

Dwarf Bunting
*Emberiza pusilla* Pallas
Family *Emberizidae*
Order *Passeriformes*
Male bird.
1870

CRITHOPHAGA MILIARIA.

Corn Bunting
*Emberiza calandra calandra* L.
Family *Emberizidae*
Order *Passeriformes*
Male bird.
1869

Ortolan Bunting
*Emberiza hortulana* L.
Family *Emberizidae*
Order *Passeriformes*
Male (left) with female.
1866

Black-headed Bunting
*Emberiza melanocephala*-Scopoli
Family *Emberizidae*
Order *Passeriformes*
Male (above) with female.
1872

SCHŒNICOLA ARUNDINACEA.

CENTROPHANES LAPPONICA.

Reed Bunting

*Emberiza schoeniclus schoeniclus* (L.)
Family *Emberizidae*
Order *Passeriformes*

Male (left) with female.
1865

Lapland Bunting

*Calcarius lapponicus lapponicus* (L.)
Family *Emberizidae*
Order *Passeriformes*

Male (above right) with young
birds in the nest (centre) and
female (left).
1867

House Sparrow (opposite)

*Passer domesticus domesticus* (L.)
Subfamily *Passerinae*
Family *Ploceidae*
Order *Passeriformes*

Male (foreground) with female
sitting on eggs in nest behind.
1863

PLECTROPHANES NIVALIS.

PASSER MONTANUS.

Snow Bunting
*Plectrophenax nivalis nivalis* (L.)
Family *Emberizidae*
Order *Passeriformes*

Male (right) with female (left) and
young birds behind in the nest.
1868

Tree Sparrow
*Passer montanus montanus* (L.)
Subfamily *Passerinae*
Family *Ploceidae*
Order *Passeriformes*

Male (below) with female.
1863

Chaffinch

*Fringilla coelebs coelebs* L.
Subfamily *Fringillinae*
Family *Fringillidae*
Order *Passeriformes*

Male (left) with female.
1862

FRINGILLA MONTIFRINGILLA.

Brambling

*Fringilla montifringilla* L.
Subfamily *Fringillinae*
Family *Fringillidae*
Order *Passeriformes*

Male (foreground) with female
sitting on eggs in nest (above)
and adult bird in winter plumage
(left).
1862

115

Goldfinch

*Carduelis carduelis carduelis* (L.)
Subfamily *Carduelinae*
Family *Fringillidae*
Order *Passeriformes*

Male (right) with female.
1863

Siskin

*Carduelis spinus* (L.)
Subfamily *Carduelinae*
Family *Fringillidae*
Order *Passeriformes*

Female (above right) with two males.
1867

Serin

*Serinus serinus* (L.)
Subfamily *Carduelinae*
Family *Fringillidae*
Order *Passeriformes*

Male (above) with female.
1870

LIGURINUS CHLORIS.

SERINUS HORTULANUS.

Greenfinch

*Carduelis chloris aurantiiventris*
 (Cabanis)
Subfamily *Carduelinae*
Family *Fringillidae*
Order *Passeriformes*

Adults in the nest with their
young.
1869

COCCOTHRAUSTES VULGARIS.

PYRRHULA VULGARIS.

Hawfinch

*Coccothraustes coccothraustes
coccothraustes* (L.)
Subfamily *Carduelinae*
Family *Fringillidae*
Order *Passeriformes*

Male (right) with male in winter
plumage (below right) and young
bird (left).
1862

Bullfinch

*Pyrrhula pyrrhula europaea* Vieillot
Subfamily *Carduelinae*
Family *Fringillidae*
Order *Passeriformes*

Male (above) with female by nest
with eggs.
1867

PYRRHULA VULGARIS.

Bullfinch
*Pyrrhula pyrrhula europaea* Vieillot
Subfamily *Carduelinae*
Family *Fringillidae*
Order *Passeriformes*

Young birds.
1873

CARPODACUS ERYTHRINUS.

Scarlet Grosbeak
*Carpodacus erythrinus erythrinus*
 (Pallas)
Subfamily *Carduelinae*
Family *Fringillidae*
Order *Passeriformes*

Male (above) with female.
1871

Crossbill

*Loxia curvirostra curvirostra* L.
Subfamily *Carduelinae*
Family *Fringillidae*
Order *Passeriformes*

Male (left) with female feeding
her young.
1864

LOXIA CURVIROSTRA, *Linn*

Pine Grosbeak

*Pinicola enucleator enucleator* (L.)
Subfamily *Carduelinae*
Family *Fringillidae*
Order *Passeriformes*

Male (above) with female.
1867

PINICOLA ENUCLEATOR.

Two-barred Crossbill
*Loxia leucoptera bifasciata* (C.L.
 Brehm)
Subfamily *Carduelinae*
Family *Fringillidae*
Order *Passeriformes*

Male (below) with female.
1864

Parrot Crossbill
*Loxia pytyopsittacus* Borkhausen
Subfamily *Carduelinae*
Family *Fringillidae*
Order *Passeriformes*

Male (above) with female.
1864

LOXIA LEUCOPTERA, *Gmel.*

LINOTA CANNABINA

American White-winged Crossbill
*Loxia leucoptera americana*
Family *Fringillidae*
Order *Passeriformes*
Male (below) with female.

Linnet
*Acanthis cannabina cannabina* (L.)
Subfamily *Carduelinae*
Family *Fringillidae*
Order *Passeriformes*
Male in summer plumage (below left) with male in winter plumage (above) and female (right).
1868

Twite

*Acanthis flavirostris flavirostris* (L.)
Subfamily *Carduelinae*
Family *Fringillidae*
Order *Passeriformes*

Male (right) with female.
1865

Redpoll

*Acanthis flammea flammea* (L.)
Subfamily *Carduelinae*
Family *Fringillidae*
Order *Passeriformes*

Female (below) with males of the
Scandinavian species (above and
left).
1866

ÆGIOTHUS RUFESCENS.

Lesser Redpoll
*Acanthis flammea cabaret* (Müller)
Subfamily *Carduelinae*
Family *Fringillidae*
Order *Passeriformes*
Male (left) with female by her
eggs.
1866

STURNUS VULGARIS, *Linn.*
Young.

Starling
*Sturnus vulgaris vulgaris* (L.)
Family *Sturnidae*
Order *Passeriformes*
Young birds at different stages of
development.
1873

Starling (opposite)
*Sturnus vulgaris vulgaris* (L.)
Family *Sturnidae*
Order *Passeriformes*
Male (right) with female by her
young in the nest-cavity.
1868

PASTOR ROSEUS.

PASTOR ROSEUS.

Rose-coloured Pastor
*Sturnus roseus* (L.)
Family *Sturnidae*
Order *Passeriformes*
Male (left) with female.
1865

Rose-coloured Pastor
*Sturnus roseus* (L.)
Family *Sturnidae*
Order *Passeriformes*
Young bird.
1873

CORVUS CORAX, *Linn*

CORVUS CORONE, *Linn*

Raven

*Corvus corax corax* L.
Family *Corvidae*
Order *Passeriformes*

Male.
1867

Carrion Crow

*Corvus corone corone* L.
Family *Corvidae*
Order *Passeriformes*

Adult birds.
1870

CORVUS CORNIX, *Linn*

Hooded Crow

*Corvus corone cornix* L.
Family *Corvidae*
Order *Passeriformes*

Adult bird preying on a clutch of
eggs from a partridge's nest.
1870

Rook

*Corvus frugilegus frugilegus* L.
Family *Corvidae*
Order *Passeriformes*

Adult bird.
1864

CORVUS FRUGILEGUS, *Linn*

CORVUS MONEDULA, *Linn*.

FREGILUS GRACULUS.

Jackdaw

*Corvus monedula spermologus*
 (Vieillot)
Family *Corvidae*
Order *Passeriformes*

Adult birds.
1866

Chough

*Pyrrhocorax pyrrhocorax*
 *erythrorhamphus* (Vieillot)
Family *Corvidae*
Order *Passeriformes*

Male (right) with female sitting
on eggs in the nest.
1871

PICA CAUDATA.

GARRULUS GLANDARIUS.

Magpie
*Pica pica pica* (L.)
Family *Corvidae*
Order *Passeriformes*
Adult birds.
1862

Jay
*Garrulus glandarius glandarius* (L.)
Family *Corvidae*
Order *Passeriformes*
Male (foreground) with female.
1862

Nutcracker (opposite)
*Nucifraga caryocatactes caryocatactes*
 (L.)
Family *Corvidae*
Order *Passeriformes*
Adult birds.
1865

NUCIFRAGA CARYOCATACTES.
Young.

CUCULUS CANORUS, Linn.

Nutcracker
*Nucifraga caryocatactes caryocatactes*
 (L.)
Family *Corvidae*
Order *Passeriformes*
Young bird.
1873

Cuckoo
*Cuculus canorus canorus* L.
Subfamily *Cuculinae*
Family *Cuculidae*
Order *Cuculiformes*
Male (foreground) with young
Cuckoo being fed by a White
Wagtail.
1864

CUCULUS CANORUS.

Young ejecting its nestling Companions.
(See Introductory article Cuculus Canorus.)

OXYLOPHUS GLANDARIUS.

Cuckoo

*Cuculus canorus canorus* (L.)
Subfamily *Cuculinae*
Family *Cuculidae*
Order *Cuculiformes*

Meadow Pipit's nest parasitized
by Cuckoo, with young Cuckoo
expelling the Meadow Pipit's
fledgelings from the nest.
1873

Great Spotted Cuckoo

*Clamator glandarius* (L.)
Subfamily *Cuculinae*
Family *Cuculidae*
Order *Cuculiformes*

Male bird.
1871

White-backed Woodpecker
*Dendrocopos leucotos leucotos*
 (Bechstein)
Subfamily *Picinae*
Family *Picidae*
Order *Piciformes*
Adult birds.
1873

PICUS LEUCONOTUS, *Bechst.*

Great Spotted Woodpecker
*Dendrocopos major major* (L.)
Subfamily *Picinae*
Family *Picidae*
Order *Piciformes*
Male (right) with female (centre)
and young male bird (left).
1863

PICUS MAJOR, *Linn.*

Great Black Woodpecker
*Dryocopus martius martius* (L.)
Subfamily *Picinae*
Family *Picidae*
Order *Piciformes*
Male (left) with female in the
nest-cavity.
1871

Lesser Spotted Woodpecker
*Dendrocopos minor buturlini*
 (Hartert)
Subfamily *Picinae*
Family *Picidae*
Order *Piciformes*
Female (right) with male by the
nest-cavity with their young.
1863

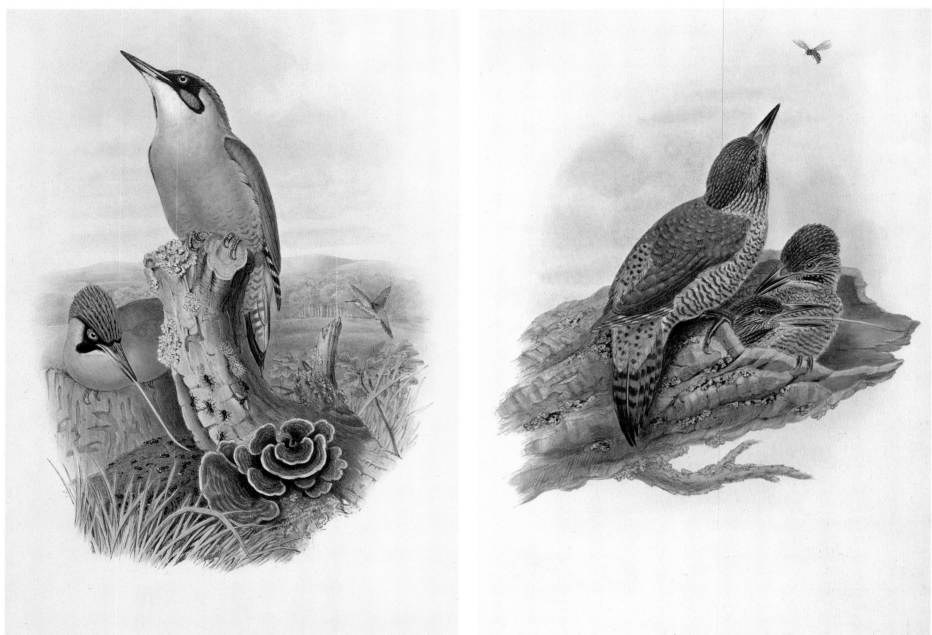

GECINUS VIRIDIS.

GECINUS VIRIDIS.
Young

Green Woodpecker
*Picus viridis pronus* Hartert
Subfamily *Picinae*
Family *Picidae*
Order *Piciformes*
Male (right) with female feeding
on ants.
1873

Green Woodpecker
*Picus viridis pronus* Hartert
Subfamily *Picinae*
Family *Picidae*
Order *Piciformes*
Young birds.
1873

YUNX TORQUILLA.

Wryneck
*Jynx torquilla torquilla* (L.)
Subfamily *Jynginae*
Family *Picidae*
Order *Piciformes*
Male (below) with female.
1862

# Rasores
Pigeons and their Allies, Gallinaceous Birds,
and Bustards

# and
# Grallatores
Cranes, Herons and their Allies, Waders,
and Rails

PALUMBUS TORQUATUS.

J.Gould & H.C.Richter del. et lith.    Walter Imp.

COLUMBA ŒNAS, Linn.

J.Gould and H.C.Richter del. et lith.    Walter Imp.

Wood Pigeon
*Columba palumbus palumbus* L.
Family *Columbidae*
Order *Columbiformes*
Adult bird.
1868

Stock Dove
*Columba oenas oenas* (L.)
Family *Columbidae*
Order *Columbiformes*
Male (foreground) with female.
1866

COLUMBA LIVIA, *Temm*

TURTUR AURITUS, *Ray*

Rock Pigeon
*Columba livia livia* Gmelin
Family *Columbidae*
Order *Columbiformes*
Adult birds, in the background
sitting in nests.
1870

Turtle Dove
*Streptopelia turtur turtur* (L.)
Family *Columbidae*
Order *Columbiformes*
Male (right) with female sitting
on eggs.
1870

Capercaillie
*Tetrao urogallus urogallus* L.
Family *Tetraonidae*
Order *Galliformes*

Male with female seen
from behind.
1872

Black Grouse
*Lyrurus tetrix tetrix* (L.)
Family *Tetraonidae*
Order *Galliformes*

Male (right) with female (left)
and males fighting in the
background.
1871

TETRAO TETRIX, *Linn.*

Red Grouse

*Lagopus lagopus scoticus* (L.)
Family *Tetraonidae*
Order *Galliformes*

Adult bird with young.
1873

Rock Ptarmigan

*Lagopus mutus helveticus*
 (Thienemann)
Family *Tetraonidae*
Order *Galliformes*

Adult birds in their winter plumage, squatting in the background, to camouflage themselves from the eyes of the Golden Eagle.
1864

LAGOPUS MUTUS.
Summer plumage.

J.Wolf and H.C.Richter del et lith.          Walter & Cohn. Imp.

Rock Ptarmigan

*Lagopus mutus helveticus*
 (Thienemann)
Family *Tetraonidae*
Order *Galliformes*

Male in summer plumage
(foreground) with female in
summer plumage with her young.
1864

Rock Ptarmigan

*Lagopus mutus helveticus*
 (Thienemann)
Family *Tetraonidae*
Order *Galliformes*

Female in autumn plumage
(foreground) with young birds.
1864

LAGOPUS MUTUS.
Autumn plumage.

J.Wolf and H.C.Richter. del et lith.          Walter & Cohn. Imp.

SYRRHAPTES PARADOXUS.

Pallas's Sandgrouse

*Syrrhaptes paradoxus* (Pallas)
Family *Pteroclidae*
Order *Columbiformes*

Male (left) with female with
clutch of eggs.
1863

Pheasant

*Phasianus colchicus colchicus* (L.)
Family *Phasianidae*
Order *Galliformes*

Male killed by a snare, with male
and female behind.
1873

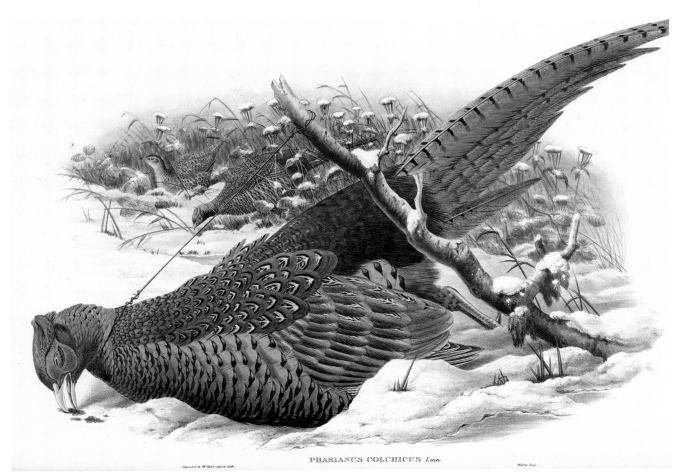

PHASIANUS COLCHICUS Linn.

Great Bustard
*Otis tarda tarda* (L.)
Family *Otididae*
Order *Gruiformes*
Female with two young
(foreground) with males in
courtship display behind.
1864

Little Bustard
*Otis tetrax tetrax* (L.)
Family *Otididae*
Order *Gruiformes*
Male (right) with female, with
another male in courtship display
behind.
1864

Crane

*Grus grus grus*
Family *Gruidae*
Order *Gruiformes*

Adult bird (foreground) with
adult birds gathered together
for migration, and V-shaped
migratory formation above.
1873

Grey Heron

*Ardea cinerea cinerea* L.
Family *Ardeidae*
Order *Ciconiiformes*

Adult birds with their young in
the nest.
1865

PERDIX CINEREA, *Linn.*

Grey Partridge
*Perdix perdix italica* Hartert
Family *Phasianidae*
Order *Galliformes*

Male (left) with female.
1871

Red-legged Partridge
*Alectoris rufa rufa* (L.)
Family *Phasianidae*
Order *Galliformes*

Adult birds (foreground) with
young birds.
1868

CACCABIS RUBRA.

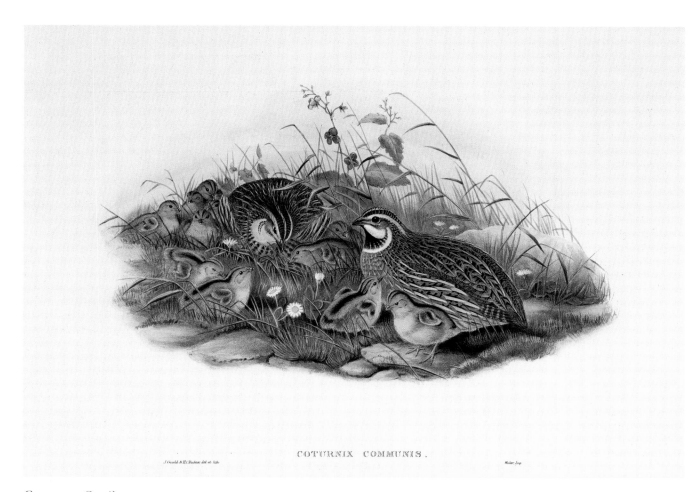

COTURNIX COMMUNIS.

Common Quail

*Coturnix coturnix coturnix* (L.)
Family *Phasianidae*
Order *Galliformes*

Male (right) with female with
their young.
1871

Little Button Quail

*Turnix sylvatica sylvatica*
 (Desfontaines)
Family *Turnicidae*
Order *Gruiformes*

Male (right) with female.
1871

TURNIX AFRICANUS, *Desf.*

149

ARDEA PURPUREA, Linn.

Purple Heron
*Ardea purpurea purpurea* L.
Family *Ardeidae*
Order *Ciconiiformes*
Adult bird sitting on eggs in nest.
1873

Great White Egret
*Egretta alba alba* (L.)
Family *Ardeidae*
Order *Ciconiiformes*
Adult bird in summer plumage
(foreground) with adult bird in
winter plumage.
1873

HERODIAS ALBA.

Little Egret

*Egretta garzetta garzetta* (L.)
Family *Ardeidae*
Order *Ciconiiformes*

Adult birds in summer plumage.
1870

HERODIAS GARZETTA.

Cattle Egret

*Bubulcus ibis ibis* (L.)
Family *Ardeidae*
Order *Ciconiiformes*

Adult bird in summer plumage
(foreground) with young birds.
1871

BUBULCUS RUSSATUS.

BUPHUS COMATUS.

Squacco Heron
*Ardeola ralloides* (Scopoli)
Family *Ardeidae*
Order *Ciconiiformes*
Adult birds in summer
plumage.
1866

Night Heron
*Nycticorax nycticorax nycticorax*
 (L.)
Family *Ardeidae*
Order *Ciconiiformes* ·
Adult (foreground) with young
bird.
1870

NYCTICORAX GRISEUS.

BOTAURUS STELLARIS.

Bittern

*Botaurus stellaris stellaris* (L.)
Family *Ardeidae*
Order *Ciconiiformes*

Adult bird with its young in
the nest.
1864

American Bittern

*Botaurus lentiginosus lentiginosus*
  (L.)
Family *Ardeidae*
Order *Ciconiiformes*

Adult bird.
1872

BOTAURUS LENTIGINOSUS.

ARDETTA MINUTA.

Little Bittern
*Ixobrychus minutus minutus* (L.)
Family *Ardeidae*
Order *Ciconiiformes*
Male (foreground) with female.
1871

Spoonbill
*Platalea leucorodia leucorodia* L.
Family *Threskiornithidae*
Order *Ciconiiformes*
Male with young in the nest,
and female behind.
1868

PLATALEA LEUCORODIA. *Linn.*

White Stork

*Ciconia ciconia ciconia* (L.)
Family *Ciconiidae*
Order *Ciconiiformes*

Adult bird feeds its young in
the nest.
1871

Black Stork

*Ciconia nigra* (L.)
Family *Ciconiidae*
Order *Ciconiiformes*

Adult birds.
1871

Lapwing

*Vanellus vanellus* (L.)
Family *Charadriidae*
Order *Charadriiformes*

Adult bird with young.
1865

Black-winged Stilt

*Himantopus himantopus
  himantopus* (L.)
Family *Recurvirostridae*
Order *Charadriiformes*

Male (foreground) with female
and young.
1870

OEDICNEMUS CREPITANS.

Stone Curlew

*Burhinus oedicnemus oedicnemus*
  (L.)
Family *Burhinidae*
Order *Charadriiformes*

Adult bird with young.
1869

Black-bellied Plover

*Pluvialis squatarola* (L.)
Family *Charadriidae*
Order *Charadriiformes*

Adult birds in summer
plumage.
1872

SQUATAROLA HELVETICA.

SQUATAROLA HELVETICA.
Plumage of Winter and young of the year

Black-bellied Plover

*Pluvialis squatarola* (L.)
Family *Charadriidae*
Order *Charadriiformes*
Adult bird in winter plumage (left)
with young bird.
1872

Golden Plover

*Pluvialis apricaria apricaria* (L.)
Family *Charadriidae*
Order *Charadriiformes*
Adult birds in winter plumage.
1864

CHARADRIUS PLUVIALIS, Linn.
Winter plumage

Golden Plover

*Pluvialis apricaria apricaria* (L.)
Family *Charadriidae*
Order *Charadriiformes*

Adult birds in summer plumage
with their young.
1864

ÆGIALOPHILUS CANTIANUS.

Kentish Plover
*Charadrius alexandrinus*
  *alexandrinus* L.
Family *Charadriidae*
Order *Charadriiformes*
Male (right) with female and
young.
1875

Ringed Plover
*Charadrius hiaticula hiaticula* L.
Family *Charadriidae*
Order *Charadriiformes*
Adult bird with young.
1873

ÆGIALITIS HIATICULA.

AEGIALITIS MINOR.

Little Ringed Plover
*Charadrius dubius curonicus*
  Gmelin
Family *Charadriidae*
Order *Charadriiformes*
Adults with clutch of eggs.
1871

Dotterel
*Eudromias morinellus* (L.)
Family *Charadriidae*
Order *Charadriiformes*
Male (right) with female.
1862

EUDROMIAS MORINELLUS.

CURSORIUS GALLICUS.

Cream-coloured Courser

*Cursorius cursor cursor* (Latham)
Family *Glareolidae*
Order *Charadriiformes*

Adult birds (right and left)
with young bird (centre).
1866

HÆMATOPUS OSTRALEGUS, *Linn*

Oystercatcher

*Haematopus ostralegus ostralegus*
L.
Family *Haematopodidae*
Order *Charadriiformes*

Adult in summer plumage
(foreground) with adult in
winter plumage behind.
1870

GLAREOLA PRATINCOLA.

Pratincole
*Glareola pratincola pratincola* (L.)
Family *Glareolidae*
Order *Charadriiformes*
Adult birds with their young.
1871

Glossy Ibis
*Plegadis falcinellus* (L.)
Family *Threskiornithidae*
Order *Ciconiiformes*
Male (foreground) with two
young birds behind.
1872

FALCINELLUS IGNEUS.

Curlew
*Numenius arquata arquata* (L.)
Family *Scolopacidae*
Order *Charadriiformes*
Adult bird with young.
1869

NUMENIUS ARQUATA.

NUMENIUS PRÆOPUS.

Whimbrel
*Numenius phaeopus phaeopus* (L.)
Family *Scolopacidae*
Order *Charadriiformes*
Male (foreground) with female.
1871

LIMOSA MELANURA, *Leisl.*

Black-tailed Godwit
*Limosa limosa limosa* (L.)
Family *Scolopacidae*
Order *Charadriiformes*
Male in moult with female behind.
1868

Bar-tailed Godwit
*Limosa lapponica lapponica* (L.)
Family *Scolopacidae*
Order *Charadriiformes*
Male in autumn plumage (right)
with female in winter plumage.
1868

LIMOSA RUFA, *Temm.*

RECURVIROSTRA AVOCETTA, *Linn.*

Avocet

*Recurvirostra avosetta avosetta* L.
Family *Recurvirostridae*
Order *Charadriiformes*

Adult bird with young.
1864

Greenshank

*Tringa nebularia* (Gunnerus)
Family *Scolopacidae*
Order *Charadriiformes*

Adult birds.
1869

GLOTTIS CANESCENS.

TOTANUS CALIDRIS.

J. Gould & H.C.Richter, del. et lith.                                        Walter. Imp.

Redshank
*Tringa totanus totanus* (L.)
Family *Scolopacidae*
Order *Charadriiformes*

Male (right) with female (left) and
young bird in autumn plumage
(centre).
1871

Spotted Redshank
*Tringa erythropus* (Pallas)
Family *Scolopacidae*
Order *Charadriiformes*

Adult in summer plumage (right)
with adult in winter plumage
(left) and young bird in autumn
plumage (centre).
1867

TOTANUS FUSCUS.

J. Gould & H.C.Richter, del. et lith.                                        Walter. Imp.

Green Sandpiper
*Tringa orchropus* L.
Family *Scolopacidae*
Order *Charadriiformes*
Adult bird with clutch of eggs
in the nest.
1865

TOTANUS OCHROPUS.

Wood Sandpiper
*Tringa glareola* L.
Family *Scolopacidae*
Order *Charadriiformes*
Male (right) with female and
young.
1868

TOTANUS GLAREOLA.

ACTITIS HYPOLEUCOS.

Common Sandpiper
*Tringa hypoleucos* L.
Family *Scolopacidae*
Order *Charadriiformes*

Adult birds with their young.
1863

Spotted Sandpiper
*Tringa macularia* (L.)
Family *Scolopacidae*
Order *Charadriiformes*

Male (centre) with female (left)
and young bird in autumn
plumage (right).
1873

ACTITIS MACULARIUS.

STREPSILAS INTERPRES.

J. Gould & H. C. Richter del. et lith.                    Walter Imp.

Turnstone

*Arenaria interpres interpres* (L.)
Family *Charadriidae*
Order *Charadriiformes*

Adult birds in courtship display,
with adult bird in non-breeding
plumage behind.
1866

Ruff

*Philomachus pugnax* (L.)
Family *Scolopacidae*
Order *Charadriiformes*

Male in nuptial plumage (right)
with female in summer plumage
(left) and males in courtship
display behind.
1871

MACHETES PUGNAX.

J. Gould & H. C. Richter del. et lith.                    Walter Imp.

MACHETES PUGNAX.

Ruff and Reeve in the plumage of the first autumn

Ruff

*Philomachus pugnax* (L.)
Family *Scolopacidae*
Order *Charadriiformes*

Young birds in autumn plumage.
1872

Upland Sandpiper

*Bartramia longicauda* (Bechstein)
Family *Scolopacidae*
Order *Charadriiformes*

Male (right) with female.
1872

ACTITURUS BARTRAMIUS.

TRYNGITES RUFESCENS.

Buff-breasted Sandpiper
*Tryngites subruficollis* (Vieillot)
Family *Scolopacidae*
Order *Charadriiformes*
Adult birds.
1865

Red Knot
*Calidris canutus canutus* (L.)
Family *Scolopacidae*
Order *Charadriiformes*
Male in summer plumage (centre)
with female in autumn plumage
(right) and young bird (left).
1873

TRINGA CANUTUS, Linn.

CALIDRIS ARENARIA.

J. Gould & H. C. Richter del. et lith.                              Walter, Imp.

Sanderling
*Calidris alba* (Pallas)
Family *Scolopacidae*
Order *Charadriiformes*

Adult birds from left to right in
winter, summer and autumn
plumage.
1867

Pectoral Sandpiper
*Calidris melanotos* (Vieillot)
Family *Scolopacidae*
Order *Charadriiformes*

Adult birds.
1870

J. Gould & H. C. Richter del. et lith.          LIMNOCINCLUS PECTORALIS.          Walter, Imp.

ANCYLOCHEILUS SUBARQUATA.

Curlew Sandpiper
*Calidris ferruginea* (Pontoppidan)
Family *Scolopacidae*
Order *Charadriiformes*

Adult bird in summer plumage
(right) with female in winter
plumage.
1872

Dunlin
*Calidris alpina alpina* (L.)
Family *Scolopacidae*
Order *Charadriiformes*

Adult birds in summer plumage
with their young.
1867

PELIDNA CINCLUS.
(Summer plumage)

PELIDNA CINCLUS.
(Winter plumage)

Dunlin
*Calidris alpina alpina* (L.)
Family *Scolopacidae*
Order *Charadriiformes*
Adult birds in winter plumage.
1867

White-rumped Sandpiper
*Calidris fuscicollis* (Vieillot)
Family *Scolopacidae*
Order *Charadriiformes*
Adult birds in moult.
1873

PELIDNA BONAPARTEI.

Little Stint
*Calidris minuta* (Leisler)
Family *Scolopacidae*
Order *Charadriiformes*

Male (right) with female
in summer plumage.
1870

ACTODROMAS MINUTA.

LEIMONITES TEMMINCKI.

Temminck's Stint
*Calidris temminckii* (Leisler)
Family *Scolopacidae*
Order *Charadriiformes*

Adult birds with young.
1870

ARQUATELLA MARITIMA.

Purple Sandpiper

*Calidris maritima* (Brunnich)
Family *Scolopacidae*
Order *Charadriiformes*

Adult birds in winter plumage
(foreground) with birds in moult
behind.

Least Sandpiper

*Calidris minutilla*
Family *Scolopacidae*
Order *Charadriiformes*

Adult birds, in summer plumage
(left and centre) and winter
plumage (right).
1870

LIMICOLA PYGMÆA.

MACRORAMPHUS GRISEUS.

Brown Snipe

*Limnodromus scolopaceus* (Say)
Family *Scolopacidae*
Order *Charadriiformes*

Adult bird in summer plumage
(right) with bird in moult.
1872

Woodcock

*Scolopax rusticola* L.
Family *Scolopacidae*
Order *Charadriiformes*

Female with young (foreground)
and male behind.
1866

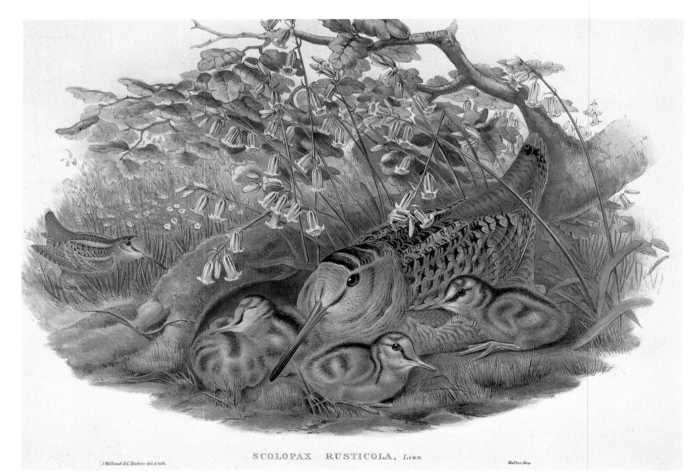

SCOLOPAX RUSTICOLA, *Linn.*

GALLINAGO MAJOR.

Great Snipe
*Gallinago media* (Latham)
Family *Scolopacidae*
Order *Charadriiformes*

Male (left) with female half-
hidden.
1863

Common Snipe
*Gallinago gallinago gallinago* (L.)
Family *Scolopacidae*
Order *Charadriiformes*

Male (right) with female and their
young.
1863

GALLINAGO SCOLOPACINUS.

Jack Snipe
*Lymnocryptes minimus* (Brünnich)
Family *Scolopacidae*
Order *Charadriiformes*
Female (left) with male.
1865

Grey Phalarope
*Phalaropus fulicarius* (L.)
Family *Phalaropodidae*
Order *Charadriiformes*
Male in summer plumage (left) with female.
1866

PHALAROPUS FULICARIUS.
Winter plumage

Grey Phalarope
*Phalaropus fulicarius* (L.)
Family *Phalaropodidae*
Order *Charadriiformes*
Adult birds in winter plumage.
1866

LOBIPES HYPERBOREUS.

Red-necked Phalarope
*Phalaropus lobatus* (L.)
Family *Phalaropodidae*
Order *Charadriiformes*
Male (right) with young and
female behind.
1866

FULICA ATRA.

Coot
*Fulica atra atra* L.
Family *Rallidae*
Order *Gruiformes*
Male (foreground) with female
and their young in the nest.
1862

Moorhen
*Gallinula chloropus chloropus* (L.)
Family *Rallidae*
Order *Gruiformes*
Adult birds with their young.
1862

GALLINULA CHLOROPUS.

RALLUS AQUATICUS, *Linn.*

Water Rail
*Rallus aquaticus aquaticus* L.
Family *Rallidae*
Order *Gruiformes*

Male (left) with female and her
young.
1863

Corn Crake
*Crex crex* (L.)
Family *Rallidae*
Order *Gruiformes*

Male with young (foreground)
with female half-hidden behind.
1863

CREX PRATENSIS.

PORZANA MARUETTA.

Spotted Crake

*Porzana porzana* (L.)
Family *Rallidae*
Order *Gruiformes*

Male (left) with female and their
young.
1864

Baillon's Crake
*Porzana pusilla intermedia*
 (Hermann)
Family *Rallidae*
Order *Gruiformes*

Adult birds.
1864

PORZANA PYGMÆA.

PORZANA MINUTA.

Little Crake

*Porzana parva* (Scopoli)
Family *Rallidae*
Order *Gruiformes*

Male (right) with female.
1864

# Natatores
## Waterfowl and Sea Birds

ANSER FERUS, Steph.

Grey Lag Goose

*Anser anser anser* (L.)
Family *Anatidae*
Order *Anseriformes*

Wounded male (foreground) with flock of migrating birds.
1873

Bean Goose

*Anser fabalis fabalis* (Latham)
Family *Anatidae*
Order *Anseriformes*

Male bird.
1873

ANSER SEGETUM.

ANSER BRACHYRHYNCHUS, Baill.

Pink-footed Goose
*Anser fabalis brachyrhynchus*
  Baillon
Family *Anatidae*
Order *Anseriformes*
Male (foreground) with female.
1871

White-fronted Goose
*Anser albifrons albifrons* (Scopoli)
Family *Anatidae*
Order *Anseriformes*
Adult bird with young.
1871

ANSER ALBIFRONS.

Barnacle Goose
*Branta leucopsis* (Bechstein)
Family *Anatidae*
Order *Anseriformes*
Adult birds.
1867

BERNICLA LEUCOPSIS.

BERNICLA RUFICOLLIS.

Red-breasted Goose
*Branta ruficollis* (Pallas)
Family *Anatidae*
Order *Anseriformes*
Adult (foreground) with young bird.
1870

BERNICLA BRENTA.

Brent Goose

*Branta bernicla bernicla* (L.)
Family *Anatidae*
Order *Anseriformes*

Dark-phased birds.
1870

Mute Swan

*Cygnus olor* (Gmelin)
Family *Anatidae*
Order *Anseriformes*

Male (foreground) with female
and her young.
1872

CYGNUS OLOR.

CYGNUS FERUS.

Whooper Swan
*Cygnus cygnus* (L.)
Family *Anatidae*
Order *Anseriformes*
Adult bird.
1872

Bewick's Swan
*Cygnus bewickii* Yarrell
Family *Anatidae*
Order *Anseriformes*
Adult bird.
1872

CYGNUS MINOR.

TADORNA VULPANSER.

Shelduck

*Tadorna tadorna* (L.)
Family *Anatidae*
Order *Anseriformes*

Male with young (foreground)
and female in flight.
1869

Ruddy Shelduck

*Tadorna ferruginea* (Pallas)
Family *Anatidae*
Order *Anseriformes*

Male (foreground) with female.
1869

CASARCA RUTILA.

MARECA PENELOPE.

Widgeon
*Anas penelope* L.
Family *Anatidae*
Order *Anseriformes*
Male (foreground) with female.
1871

Shoveller Duck
*Anas clypeata* L.
Family *Anatidae*
Order *Anseriformes*
Males (left and right) with female (centre).
1871

SPATULA CLYPEATA.

ANAS BOSCHAS, *Linn.*

Mallard
*Anas platyrhynchos platyrhynchos*
 L.
Family *Anatidae*
Order *Anseriformes*
Male (left) with female.
1872

Teal
*Anas crecca crecca* L.
Family *Anatidae*
Order *Anseriformes*
Male with young, and female
in the background.
1865

QUERQUEDULA CRECCA.

QUERQUEDULA CIRCIA.

Garganey

*Anas querquedula* L.
Family *Anatidae*
Order *Anseriformes*

Male (foreground) with males and
one female (right) taking flight.
1865

Pintail

*Anas acuta acuta* L.
Family *Anatidae*
Order *Anseriformes*

Males (foreground) with female.
1869

DAFILA ACUTA.

CHAULELASMUS STREPERA.

Gadwall

*Anas strepera strepera* L.
Family *Anatidae*
Order *Anseriformes*

Male (foreground) with female.
1868

Pochard

*Aythya ferina* (L.)
Family *Anatidae*
Order *Anseriformes*

Male (foreground) with female.
1871

NYROCA FERINA.

NYROCA LEUCOPHTHALMOS.

White-eyed Pochard

*Aythya nyroca* (Güldenstädt)
Family *Anatidae*
Order *Anseriformes*

Male (foreground) with female.
1872

Red-crested duck

*Netta rufina* (Pallas)
Family *Anatidae*
Order *Anseriformes*

Male (foreground) with female.
1867

BRANTA RUFINA.

FULIGULA CRISTATA.

Tufted Duck
*Aythya fuligula* (L.)
Family *Anatidae*
Order *Anseriformes*

Male (foreground) with female.
1871

Scaup Duck
*Aythya marila marila* (L.)
Family *Anatidae*
Order *Anseriformes*

Male (right) with female.
1869

FULIGULA MARILA.

Steller's Eider
*Polysticta stelleri* (L.)
Family *Anatidae*
Order *Anseriformes*

Males (left and right) with female
(centre).
1863

Common Eider
*Somateria mollissima mollissima* (L.)
Family *Anatidae*
Order *Anseriformes*

Male (foreground) with male
(right) and female.
1870

SOMATERIA SPECTABILIS.

J.Gould & H.C.Richter, del et lith.                                    Walter Imp.

King Eider
*Somateria spectabilis* (L.)
Family *Anatidae*
Order *Anseriformes*
Male (left) with female.
1870

Black Scoter
*Melanitta nigra nigra* (L.)
Family *Anatidae*
Order *Anseriformes*
Males (foreground and right) with female.
1862

OIDEMIA NIGRA.

OIDEMIA FUSCA.

Velvet Scoter
*Melanitta fusca fusca* (L.)
Family *Anatidae*
Order *Anseriformes*
Male (right) with female and
their young.
1867

Surf Scoter
*Melanitta perspicillata* (L.)
Family *Anatidae*
Order *Anseriformes*
Two males (foreground) with
female.
1867

OIDEMIA PERSPICILLATA.

CLANGULA GLAUCION.

J. Gould & H.C. Richter del et lith.    Walter Imp.

Goldeneye

*Bucephala clangula clangula* (L.)
Family *Anatidae*
Order *Anseriformes*

Female (foreground) with male,
and two males in courtship
display in the background.
1869

Harlequin Duck

*Histrionicus histrionicus* (L.)
Family *Anatidae*
Order *Anseriformes*

Male (foreground) with female.
1869

HISTRIONICUS TORQUATUS.

J. Gould & H.C. Richter del et lith.    Walter Imp.

HARELDA GLACIALIS.

Long-tailed Duck

*Clangula hyemalis* (L.)
Family *Anatidae*
Order *Anseriformes*

Male in winter plumage
(foreground) with male (centre)
and female (right) in summer
plumage.
1870

Goosander

*Mergus merganser merganser* L.
Family *Anatidae*
Order *Anseriformes*

Male (foreground) with female
and Kingfisher in the
background.
1866

MERGUS CASTOR, *Linn*

MERGUS SERRATOR.

Red-breasted Merganser

*Mergus serrator* L.
Family *Anatidae*
Order *Anseriformes*

Male (right) with female and
her young.
1862

Hooded Merganser

*Mergus cucullatus* (L.)
Family *Anatidae*
Order *Anseriformes*

In the foreground and in the
background on the right,
female previously believed to
belong to another species,
known as *Lophodytes cucullatus.*
1866

MERGUS CUCULLATUS. *Linn*

MERGUS ALBELLUS.

Smew

*Mergus albellus* L.
Family *Anatidae*
Order *Anseriformes*

Males (foreground) with
female.
1862

Great-crested Grebe

*Podiceps cristatus cristatus* (L.)
Family *Podicipedidae*
Order *Podicipediformes*

Adult bird swimming with
newly-born young on its back.
1863

PODICEPS CRISTATUS, *latter*

Red-necked Grebe
*Podiceps grisegena grisegena*
(Boddaert)
Family *Podicipedidae*
Order *Podicipediformes*
Male (left) with female.
1863

PODICEPS RUBRICOLLIS.

Horned Grebe

*Podiceps auritus auritus* (L.)
Family *Podicipedidae*
Order *Podicipediformes*

Male (left) with female with
clutch of eggs, and behind,
perched on a reed mace a male
Bearded Tit.
1870

PODICEPS AURITUS.

PODICEPS NIGRICOLLIS.

Black-necked Grebe
*Podiceps nigricollis nigricollis* C.L.
  Brehm
Family *Podicipedidae*
Order *Podicipediformes*
Male (foreground) with female.
1863

Little Grebe
*Podiceps ruficollis ruficollis* (Pallas)
Family *Podicipedidae*
Order *Podicipediformes*
Male (left) with female (right) and
their young (centre).
1862

PODICEPS MINOR.

COLYMBUS GLACIALIS, *Linn.*

Great Northern Diver

*Gavia immer* (Brünnich)
Family *Gaviidae*
Order *Gaviiformes*

Adult bird in summer plumage.
1865

Black-throated Diver

*Gavia arctica arctica* (L.)
Family *Gaviidae*
Order *Gaviiformes*

Adult birds in their summer
plumage.
1865

COLYMBUS ARCTICUS, *Linn.*

COLYMBUS SEPTENTRIONALIS, *Linn.*

Red-throated Diver
*Gavia stellata stellata*
(Pontoppidan)
Family *Gaviidae*
Order *Gaviiformes*

Adult bird in summer plumage
with young.
1865

Great Auk
*Alca impennis* L.
Family *Alcidae*
Order *Charadriiformes*

Extinct species.
1873

ALCA IMPENNIS.

Razorbill

*Alca torda torda* L.
Family *Alcidae*
Order *Charadriiformes*

Adult bird with young bird,
with nest-building colony in
the background.
1866

Common Guillemot

*Uria aalge albionis* Witherby
Family *Alcidae*
Order *Charadriiformes*

Adult bird in nuptial plumage
with clutch of eggs
(foreground) and behind, the
species known as Bridled
Guillemot because of the white
band and eyebrow.
1873

ALCA TORDA, Linn

URIA TROÏLE.

211

URIA GRYLLE.

Black Guillemot

*Cepphus grylle* (L.)
Family *Alcidae*
Order *Charadriiformes*

Adult bird in winter plumage
(left) with adult bird in summer
plumage.
1869

Little Auk

*Plotus alle alle* (L.)
Family *Alcidae*
Order *Charadriiformes*

Adult bird in summer plumage
(right) with adult bird in winter
plumage.
1868

MERGULUS ALLE.

Puffin

*Fratercula arctica grabae* (C.L.
 Brehm)
Family *Alcidae*
Order *Charadriiformes*

Adult bird feeding young bird.
1865

PHALACROCORAX CARBO.

PHALACROCORAX GRACULUS.

Cormorant

*Phalacrocorax carbo carbo* (L.)
Family *Phalacrocoracidae*
Order *Pelecaniformes*

Male (foreground) with female of
the Atlantic variety in summer
plumage sitting on eggs.
1873

Shag

*Phalacrocorax aristotelis aristotelis*
 (L.)
Family *Phalacrocoracidae*
Order *Pelecaniformes*

Adult bird in summer plumage
with newly-born young.
1872

SULA BASSANA, *Linn.*

Gannet

*Sula bassana bassana* (L.)
Family *Sulidae*
Order *Pelecaniformes*

Adult bird (foreground) with nest-building colony and young.
1873

Great Black-backed Gull

*Larus marinus* L.
Subfamily *Larinae*
Family *Laridae*
Order *Charadriiformes*

Adult bird (foreground) with young birds in flight.
1873

LARUS MARINUS, *Linn.*

LARUS FUSCUS, *Linn.*

Lesser Black-backed Gull

*Larus fuscus fuscus* L.
Subfamily *Larinae*
Family *Laridae*
Order *Charadriiformes*

Adult bird in summer plumage
(foreground) with young bird in
its first winter plumage (behind).
1871

Glaucous Gull

*Larus hyperboreus hyperboreus*
 Gunnerus
Subfamily *Larinae*
Family *Laridae*
Order *Charadriiformes*

Adult bird in summer plumage
(foreground) with young bird in
its first winter plumage.
1873

LARUS GLAUCUS, *Brunn.*

LARUS ISLANDICUS, *Edm.*

Iceland Gull

*Larus glaucoides glaucoides* Meyer
Subfamily *Larinae*
Family *Laridae*
Order *Charadriiformes*

Adult bird in summer plumage
(foreground) with young bird in
its first winter plumage.
1873

Herring Gull

*Larus argentatus argentatus*
 Pontoppidan
Subfamily *Larinae*
Family *Laridae*
Order *Charadriiformes*

Adult birds in summer plumage
(foreground) with young bird in
winter plumage.
1873

LARUS CANUS. *Linn.*

Common Gull
*Larus canus canus* L.
Subfamily *Larinae*
Family *Laridae*
Order *Charadriiformes*

Young bird (foreground) with
adult bird in the nest.
1867

Kittiwake
*Rissa tridactyla* (L.)
Subfamily *Larinae*
Family *Laridae*
Order *Charadriiformes*

Young bird in juvenile
plumage (foreground) with
adult.
1869

*RISSA TRIDACTYLA.*

Ivory Gull

*Pagophila eburnea* (Phipps)
Subfamily *Larinae*
Family *Laridae*
Order *Charadriiformes*

Adult bird (foreground) with
young bird in juvenile
plumage.
1870

Ross's Gull

*Rhodostethia rosea* (MacGillivray)
Subfamily *Larinae*
Family *Laridae*
Order *Charadriiformes*

Adult bird in summer plumage
(foreground) with adult birds
in winter plumage.

CHROICOCEPHALUS RIDIBUNDUS.

Black-headed Gull
*Larus ridibundus* L.
Subfamily *Larinae*
Family *Laridae*
Order *Charadriiformes*
Adult bird with young.
1873

Bonaparte's Gull
*Larus philadelphia* (L.)
Subfamily *Larinae*
Family *Laridae*
Order *Charadriiformes*
Adult bird in summer plumage (right) with young bird which has almost shed its juvenile plumage.
1873

CHROICOCEPHALUS PHILADELPHIA.

HYDROCOLŒUS MINUTUS.

Little Gull

*Larus minutus* Pallas
Subfamily *Larinae*
Family *Laridae*
Order *Charadriiformes*

Adult bird in summer plumage
(left) with adult bird in winter
plumage (right) and young bird in
juvenile plumage (centre).
1869

Sabine's Gull

*Xema sabini* Sabine
Subfamily *Larinae*
Family *Laridae*
Order *Charadriiformes*

Adult bird in summer plumage
(left) with young bird in juvenile
plumage.
1866

XEMA SABINI.

HYDROPROGNE CASPIA.

Caspian Tern
*Hydroprogne tschegrava* (Lepechin)
Subfamily *Sterninae*
Family *Laridae*
Order *Charadriiformes*
Young bird in youthful plumage, with adult bird in summer plumage behind.
1873

Sandwich Tern
*Sterna sandvicensis sandvicensis*
 Lathan
Subfamily *Sterninae*
Family *Laridae*
Order *Charadriiformes*
Adult birds in summer plumage.
1872

ACTOCHELIDON CANTIACA.

Roseate Tern

*Sterna dougallii dougallii*
  Montague
Subfamily *Sterninae*
Family *Laridae*
Order *Charadriiformes*

Adult birds fighting over prey.
1867

STERNA PARADISEA, *Brünn.*

J. Gould & H.C. Richter del et lith.                    Walter, Imp.

Common Tern

*Sterna hirundo hirundo* L.
Subfamily *Sterninae*
Family *Laridae*
Order *Charadriiformes*

Adult bird feeding young.
1865

STERNA HIRUNDO, *Linn.?*

J. Gould and H.C. Richter del et lith.                    Walter, Imp.

STERNA MACRURA, *Naum.*

Arctic Tern

*Sterna paradisea* Pontoppidan
Subfamily *Sterninae*
Family *Laridae*
Order *Charadriiformes*

Adult bird (left) with young
bird in juvenile plumage.
1865

STERNULA MINUTA.

Little Tern

*Sterna albifrons albifrons* Pallas
Subfamily *Sterninae*
Family *Laridae*
Order *Charadriiformes*

Adult birds feeding their
young.
1865

GELOCHELIDON ANGLICA.

*Gelochelidon nilotica nilotica*
  (Gmelin)
Subfamily *Sterninae*
Family *Laridae*
Order *Charadriiformes*
Male (right) with young bird in juvenile plumage.
1871

Black Tern
*Chlidonias niger niger* (L.)
Subfamily *Sterninae*
Family *Laridae*
Order *Charadriiformes*
Adult birds in summer plumage (right) with young bird in moult plumage in flight.
1868

HYDROCHELIDON NIGRA.

HYDROCHELIDON LEUCOPTERA.

White-winged Black Tern

*Chlidonias leucopterus*
(Temminck)
Subfamily *Sterninae*
Family *Laridae*
Order *Charadriiformes*

Adult birds in summer
plumage
1868

Whiskered Tern

*Chlidonias hybrida hybrida* (Pallas)
Subfamily *Sterninae*
Family *Laridae*
Order *Charadriiformes*

Adult bird in summer plumage
(right) with young bird in
moult.
1868

HYDROCHELIDON LEUCOPAREIA.

STERCORARIUS CATARRAUTES.

Great Skua
*Stercorarius skua skua* (Brünnich)
Subfamily *Stercorarinae*
Family *Laridae*
Order *Charadriiformes*

Adult bird in summer plumage.
1865

Pomathorine Skua
*Stercorarius pomarinus* (Temminck)
Subfamily *Stercorarinae*
Family *Laridae*
Order *Charadriiformes*

Light-phased adult bird (right)
with young bird.
1865

STERCORARIUS POMATORHINUS.

Arctic Skua
*Stercorarius parasiticus* (L.)
Subfamily *Stercorarinae*
Family *Laridae*
Order *Charadriiformes*

Dark-phased adult bird (right)
with light-phased adult with
young.
1865

STERCORARIUS PARASITICUS.

STERCORARIUS LONGICAUDUS.

Long-tailed Skua

*Stercorarius longicaudus* Vieillot
Subfamily *Stercorarinae*
Family *Laridae*
Order *Charadriiformes*
Adult birds in summer plumage.
1865

PROCELLARIA GLACIALIS, *Linn.*

Northern Fulmar

*Fulmarus glacialis* (L.)
Family *Procellariidae*
Order *Procellariiformes*

Light-phased adult bird (right)
with dark-phased adult.
1870

Manx Shearwater

*Puffinus puffinus yelkouan* (Acerbi)
Family *Procellariidae*
Order *Procellariiformes*

Adult bird.
1870

PUFFINUS MAJOR, *Fab.*

PUFFINUS ANGLORUM.

Little Shearwater
*Puffinus assimilis baroli* (Bonaparte)
Family *Procellariidae*
Order *Procellariiformes*
Adult bird.
1868

Leach's Petrel
*Oceanodroma leucorhoa leucorhoa*
  (Vieillot)
Family *Hydrobatidae*
Order *Procellariiformes*
Adult birds.
1869

THALASSIDROMA LEACHII.

THALASSIDROMA PELAGICA.

Storm Petrel

*Hydrobates pelagicus* (L.)
Family *Hydrobatidae*
Order *Procellariiformes*

Adult birds (left and right) with
young bird in the nest (centre).
1869

# Systematic Index
## of the Species Illustrated

The order of this systematic index follows the principle generally adopted today, progressing from the less advanced to the more advanced bird families.

Order    *Gaviiformes*
Family    *Gaviidae*
Species    Red-throated Diver (*Gavia stellata stellata*)
Black-throated Diver (*Gavia arctica arctica*)
Great Northern Diver (*Gavia immer*)

Order    *Podicipediformes*
Family    *Podicipedidae*
Species    Little Grebe (*Podiceps ruficollis ruficollis*)
Black-necked Grebe (*Podiceps nigricollis nigricollis*)
Horned Grebe (*Podiceps auritus auritus*)
Red-necked Grebe (*Podiceps grisegena grisegena*)
Great Crested Grebe (*Podiceps cristatus cristatus*)

Order    *Procellariiformes*
Family    *Procellariidae*
Species    Northern Fulmar (*Fulmarus glacialis*)
Manx Shearwater (*Puffinus puffinus yelkouan*)
Little Shearwater (*Puffinus assimilis baroli*)
Family    *Hydrobatidae*
Species    Storm Petrel (*Hydrobates pelagicus*)
Leach's Storm Petrel (*Oceanodroma leucorhoa leucorhoa*)

Order    *Pelecaniformes*
Family    *Sulidae*
Species    Gannet (*Sula bassana bassana*)
Family    *Phalacrocoracidae*
Species    Cormorant (*Phalacrocorax carbo carbo*)
Shag (*Phalacrocorax aristotelis aristotelis*)

Order    *Ciconiiformes*
Family    *Ardeidae*
Species    American Bittern (*Botaurus lentiginosus lentiginosus*)
Bittern (*Botaurus stellaris stellaris*)
Little Bittern (*Ixobrychus minutus minutus*)
Night Heron (*Nycticorax nycticorax nycticorax*)
Squacco Heron (*Ardeola ralloides*)
Cattle Egret (*Bubulcus ibis ibis*)
Great White Egret (*Egretta alba alba*)
Little Egret (*Egretta garzetta garzetta*)
Grey Heron (*Ardea cinerea cinerea*)
Purple Heron (*Ardea purpurea purpurea*)
Family    *Threskiornithidae*
Species    Spoonbill (*Platalea leucorodia leucorodia*)
Glossy Ibis (*Plegadis falcinellus*)
Family    *Ciconiidae*
Species    White Stork (*Ciconia ciconia ciconia*)
Black Stork (*Ciconia nigra*)

Order    *Anseriformes*
Family    *Anatidae*
Species    Barnacle Goose (*Branta leucopsis*)
Brent Goose (*Branta bernicla bernicla*)
Red-breasted Goose (*Branta ruficollis*)
Grey Lag Goose (*Anser anser anser*)
White-fronted Goose (*Anser albifrons albifrons*)
Bean Goose (*Anser fabalis fabalis*)
Pink-footed Goose (*Anser fabalis brachyrhynchus*)
Mute Swan (*Cygnus olor*)
Whooper Swan (*Cygnus cygnus*)
Bewick's Swan (*Cygnus bewickii*)
Ruddy Shelduck (*Tadorna ferruginea*)
Shelduck (*Tadorna tadorna*)
Mallard (*Anas platyrhynchos platyrhynchos*)
Teal (*Anas crecca crecca*)
Gadwall (*Anas strepera strepera*)

Widgeon (*Anas penelope*)
Pintail (*Anas acuta acuta*)
Garganey (*Anas querquedula*)
Shoveller Duck (*Anas clypeata*)
Red-crested Duck (*Netta rufina*)
Pochard (*Aythya ferina*)
White-eyed Pochard (*Aythya nyroca*)
Tufted Duck (*Aythya fuligula*)
Scaup Duck (*Aythya marila marila*)
Steller's Eider (*Polystica stelleri*)
Common Eider (*Somateria mollissima mollissima*)
King Eider (*Somateria spectabilis*)
Black Scoter (*Melanitta nigra nigra*)
Velvet Scoter (*Melanitta fusca fusca*)
Surf Scoter (*Melanitta perspicillata*)
Harlequin Duck (*Histrionicus histrionicus*)
Long-tailed Duck (*Clangula hyemalis*)
Goldeneye (*Bucephala clangula clangula*)
Smew (*Mergus albellus*)
Red-breasted Merganser (*Mergus serrator*)
Goosander (*Mergus merganser merganser*)
Hooded Merganser (*Mergus cucullatus*)

Order    *Falconiformes*
Family    *Pandionidae*
Species    Osprey (*Pandion haliaëtus haliaëtus*)
Family    *Accipitridae*
Species    Honey Buzzard (*Pernis apivorus*)
Red Kite (*Milvus milvus milvus*)
Black Kite (*Milvus migrans migrans*)
White-tailed Eagle (*Haliaëtus albicilla*)
Goshawk (*Accipiter gentilis gentilis*)
Sparrowhawk (*Accipiter nisus nisus*)
Rough-legged Buzzard (*Buteo lagopus lagopus*)
Common Buzzard (*Buteo buteo buteo*)
Lesser Spotted Eagle (*Aquila pomarina pomarina*)
Golden Eagle (*Aquila chrysaëtos chrysaëtos*)
Egyptian Vulture (*Neophron percnopterus percnopterus*)
Hen Harrier (*Circus cyaneus cyaneus*)
Montagu's Harrier (*Circus pygargus*)
Marsh Harrier (*Circus aeruginosus aeruginosus*)
Family    *Falconidae*
Species    Gyrfalcon (*Falco rusticolus rusticolus*)
Greenland Gyrfalcon (*Falco rusticolus candicans*)
Icelandic Gyrfalcon (*Falco rusticolus islandicus*)
Peregrine Falcon (*Falco peregrinus peregrinus*)
Hobby (*Falco subbuteo subbuteo*)
Merlin (*Falco columbarius aesalon*)
Red-footed Falcon (*Falco vespertinus vespertinus*)
Kestrel (*Falco tinnunculus tinnunculus*)

Order    *Galliformes*
Family    *Tetraonidae*
Species    Rock Ptarmigan (*Lagopus mutus helveticus*)
Red Grouse (*Lagopus lagopus scoticus*)
Black Grouse (*Lyrurus tetrix tetrix*)
Capercaillie (*Tetrao urogallus urogallus*)
Family    *Phasianidae*
Species    Red-legged Partridge (*Alectoris rufa rufa*)
Grey Partridge (*Perdix perdix italica*)
Common Quail (*Coturnix coturnix coturnix*)
Pheasant (*Phasianus colchicus colchicus*)

Order    *Gruiformes*
Family    *Gruidae*
Species    Crane (*Grus grus grus*)
Family    *Otididae*
Species    Great Bustard (*Otis tarda tarda*)
Little Bustard (*Otis tetrax tetrax*)

| | |
|---|---|
| Family | *Rallidae* |
| Species | Water Rail (*Rallus aquaticus aquaticus*) |
| | Spotted Crake (*Porzana porzana*) |
| | Little Crake (*Porzana parva*) |
| | Baillon's Crake (*Porzana pusilla intermedia*) |
| | Corn Crake (*Crex crex*) |
| | Moorhen (*Gallinula chloropus chloropus*) |
| | Coot (*Fulica atra atra*) |
| Family | *Turnicidae* |
| Species | Little Button Quail (*Turnix sylvatica sylvatica*) |
| Order | *Charadriiformes* |
| Family | *Haematopodidae* |
| Species | Oystercatcher (*Haematopus ostralegus ostralegus*) |
| Family | *Charadriidae* |
| Species | Ringed Plover (*Charadrius hiaticula hiaticula*) |
| | Little Ringed Plover (*Charadrius dubius curonicus*) |
| | Kentish Plover (*Charadrius alexandrinus alexandrinus*) |
| | Dotterel (*Eudromias morinellus*) |
| | Golden Plover (*Pluvialis apricaria apricaria*) |
| | Black-bellied Plover (*Pluvialis squatarola*) |
| | Lapwing (*Vanellus vanellus*) |
| | Turnstone (*Arenaria interpres interpres*) |
| Family | *Scolopacidae* |
| Species | Little Stint (*Calidris minuta*) |
| | Temminck's Stint (*Calidris temminckii*) |
| | Least Sandpiper (*Calidris minutilla*) |
| | Pectoral Sandpiper (*Calidris melanotos*) |
| | Purple Sandpiper (*Calidris maritima*) |
| | Dunlin (*Calidris alpina alpina*) |
| | Curlew Sandpiper (*Calidris ferruginea*) |
| | Red Knot (*Calidris canutus canutus*) |
| | Sanderling (*Calidris alba*) |
| | Ruff (*Philomachus pugnax*) |
| | Buff-breasted Sandpiper (*Tryngites subruficollis*) |
| | Spotted Sandpiper (*Tringa macularia*) |
| | Upland Sandpiper (*Bartramia longicauda*) |
| | Spotted Redshank (*Tringa erythropus*) |
| | Redshank (*Tringa totanus totanus*) |
| | Greenshank (*Tringa nebularia*) |
| | Green Sandpiper (*Tringa ochropus*) |
| | White-rumped Sandpiper (*Calidris fuscicollis*) |
| | Wood Sandpiper (*Tringa glareola*) |
| | Common Sandpiper (*Tringa hypoleucos*) |
| | Brown Snipe (*Limnodromus scolopaceus*) |
| | Black-tailed Godwit (*Limosa limosa limosa*) |
| | Bar-tailed Godwit (*Limosa lapponica lapponica*) |
| | Curlew (*Numenius arquata arquata*) |
| | Whimbrel (*Numenius phaeopus phaeopus*) |
| | Woodcock (*Scolopax rusticola*) |
| | Common Snipe (*Gallinago gallinago gallinago*) |
| | Great Snipe (*Gallinago media*) |
| | Jack Snipe (*Lymnocryptes minimus*) |
| Family | *Recurvirostridae* |
| Species | Black-winged Stilt (*Himantopus himantopus himantopus*) |
| | Avocet (*Recurvirostra avosetta*) |
| Family | *Phalaropodidae* |
| Species | Grey Phalarope (*Phalaropus fulicarius*) |
| | Red-necked Phalarope (*Phalaropus lobatus*) |
| Family | *Burhinidae* |
| Species | Stone Curlew (*Burhinus oedicnemus oedicnemus*) |
| Family | *Glareolidae* |
| Species | Cream-coloured Courser (*Cursorius cursor cursor*) |
| | Pratincole (*Glareola pratincola pratincola*) |
| Family | *Laridae* |
| Subfamily | *Stercorarinae* |
| Species | Great Skua (*Stercorarius skua skua*) |
| | Pomathorine Skua (*Stercorarius pomarinus*) |
| | Arctic Skua (*Stercorarius parasiticus*) |
| | Long-tailed Skua (*Stercorarius longicaudus*) |
| Subfamily | *Larinae* |
| Species | Little Gull (*Larus minutus*) |
| | Black-headed Gull (*Larus ridibundus*) |
| | Lesser Black-backed Gull (*Larus fuscus fuscus*) |
| | Herring Gull (*Larus argentatus argentatus*) |
| | Iceland Gull (*Larus glaucoides glaucoides*) |
| | Glaucous Gull (*Larus hyperboreus hyperboreus*) |
| | Great Black-backed Gull (*Larus marinus*) |
| | Common Gull (*Larus canus canus*) |
| | Sabine's Gull (*Xema sabini*) |
| | Bonaparte's Gull (*Larus philadelphia*) |
| | Kittiwake (*Rissa tridactyla*) |

| | |
|---|---|
| | Ross's Gull (*Rhodostethia rosea*) |
| | Ivory Gull (*Pagophila eburnea*) |
| Subfamily | *Sterninae* |
| Species | Black Tern (*Chlidonias niger niger*) |
| | White-winged Black Tern (*Chlidonias leucopterus*) |
| | Whiskered Tern (*Chlidonias hybrida hybrida*) |
| | Gull-billed Tern (*Gelochelidon nilotica nilotica*) |
| | Caspian Tern (*Hydroprogne tschegrava*) |
| | Sandwich Tern (*Sterna sandvicensis sandvicensis*) |
| | Common Tern (*Sterna hirundo hirundo*) |
| | Arctic Tern (*Sterna paradisea*) |
| | Roseate Tern (*Sterna dougallii dougallii*) |
| | Little Tern (*Sterna albifrons albifrons*) |
| Family | *Alcidae* |
| Species | Little Auk (*Plotus alle alle*) |
| | Razorbill (*Alca torda torda*) |
| | Great Auk (*Alca impennis*) (Extinct) |
| | Black Guillemot (*Cepphus grylle*) |
| | Common Guillemot (*Uria aalge ablionis*) |
| | Puffin (*Fratercula arctica grabae*) |
| Order | *Columbiformes* |
| Family | *Pteroclidae* |
| | Pallas's Sandgrouse (*Syrrhaptes paradoxus*) |
| Family | *Columbidae* |
| Species | Wood Pigeon (*Columba palumbus palumbus*) |
| | Stock Dove (*Columba oenas oenas*) |
| | Rock Pigeon (*Columba livia livia*) |
| | Turtle Dove (*Streptopelia turtur turtur*) |
| Order | *Cuculiformes* |
| Family | *Cuculidae* |
| Subfamily | *Cuculinae* |
| Species | Cuckoo (*Cuculus canorus canorus*) |
| | Great Spotted Cuckoo (*Clamator glandarius*) |
| Order | *Strigiformes* |
| Family | *Strigidae* |
| Subfamily | *Striginae* |
| Species | Snowy Owl (*Nyctea scandiaca*) |
| | Eagle Owl (*Bubo bubo bubo*) |
| | Hawk Owl (*Surnia ulula*) |
| | Long-eared Owl (*Asio otus otus*) |
| | Short-eared Owl (*Asio flammeus flammeus*) |
| | Scops Owl (*Otus scops scops*) |
| | Tengmalm's Owl (*Aegolius funereus funereus*) |
| | Little Owl (*Athene noctua noctua*) |
| | Tawny Owl (*Strix aluco aluco*) |
| Subfamily | *Tytoninae* |
| Species | Barn Owl (*Tyto alba alba*) |
| Order | *Caprimulgiformes* |
| Family | *Caprimulgidae* |
| Species | Nightjar (*Caprimulgus europaeus europaeus*) |
| | Red-necked Nightjar (*Caprimulgus ruficollis ruficollis*) |
| Order | *Apodiformes* |
| Family | *Apodidae* |
| Subfamily | *Apodinae* |
| Species | Swift (*Apus apus apus*) |
| | Alpine Swift (*Apus melba melba*) |
| Order | *Coraciiformes* |
| Family | *Coraciidae* |
| Subfamily | *Coraciinae* |
| Species | Roller (*Coracias garrulus garrulus*) |
| Family | *Alcedinidae* |
| Species | Kingfisher (*Alcedo atthis ispida*) |
| Family | *Meropidae* |
| Species | Bee-eater (*Merops apiaster*) |
| Family | *Upupidae* |
| Subfamily | *Upupinae* |
| Species | Hoopoe (*Upupa epops epops*) |
| Order | *Piciformes* |
| Family | *Picidae* |
| Subfamily | *Jynginae* |
| Species | Wryneck (*Jynx torquilla torquilla*) |
| Subfamily | *Picinae* |
| Species | Green Woodpecker (*Picus viridis pronus*) |
| | Great Black Woodpecker (*Dryocopus martius martius*) |
| | Great Spotted Woodpecker (*Dendrocopos major major*) |
| | White-backed Woodpecker (*Dendrocopos leucotos leucotos*) |
| | Lesser Spotted Woodpecker (*Dendrocopos minor buturlini*) |

| | | |
|---|---|---|
| Order | *Passeriformes* | |
| Family | *Hirundinidae* | |
| Species | Sand Martin (*Riparia riparia riparia*) | |
| | Barn Swallow (*Hirundo rustica rustica*) | |
| | House Martin (*Delichon urbica urbica*) | |
| Family | *Alaudidae* | |
| Species | Short-toed Lark (*Calandrella cinerea brachydactyla*) | |
| | Calandra Lark (*Melanocorypha calandra calandra*) | |
| | White-winged Lark (*Melanocorypha leucoptera*) | |
| | Horned Lark (*Eremophila alpestris flava*) | |
| | Crested Lark (*Galerida cristata cristata*) | |
| | Wood Lark (*Lullula arborea arborea*) | |
| | Sky Lark (*Alauda arvensis arvensis*) | |
| Family | *Motacillidae* | |
| Species | Richard's Pipit (*Anthus novaeseelandiae richardi*) | |
| | Tawny Pipit (*Anthus campestris campestris*) | |
| | Tree Pipit (*Anthus trivialis trivialis*) | |
| | Meadow Pipit (*Anthus pratensis pratensis*) | |
| | Red-throated Pipit (*Anthus cervinus*) | |
| | Water Pipit (*Anthus spinoletta spinoletta*) | |
| | Rock Pipit (*Anthus spinoletta littoralis*) | |
| | Grey-headed Wagtail (*Motacilla flava flava*) | |
| | Grey-capped Wagtail (*Motacilla flava cinereocapilla*) | |
| | Spanish Wagtail (*Motacilla flava iberiae*) | |
| | Yellow Wagtail (*Motacilla flava flavissima*) | |
| | Grey Wagtail (*Motacilla cinerea cinerea*) | |
| | White Wagtail (*Motacilla alba alba*) | |
| | Pied Wagtail (*Motacilla alba yarrellii*) | |
| Family | *Laniidae* | |
| Species | Red-backed Shrike (*Lanius collurio collurio*) | |
| | Woodchat Shrike (*Lanius senator senator*) | |
| | Lesser Grey Shrike (*Lanius minor minor*) | |
| | Great Grey Shrike (*Lanius excubitor excubitor*) | |
| Family | *Oriolidae* | |
| Species | Golden Oriole (*Oriolus oriolus oriolus*) | |
| Family | *Sturnidae* | |
| Species | Rose-coloured Pastor (*Sturnus roseus*) | |
| | Starling (*Sturnus vulgaris vulgaris*) | |
| Family | *Corvidae* | |
| Species | Jay (*Garrulus glandarius glandarius*) | |
| | Magpie (*Pica pica pica*) | |
| | Nutcracker (*Nucifraga caryocatactes caryocatactes*) | |
| | Chough (*Pyrrhocorax pyrrhocorax erythrorhamphus*) | |
| | Jackdaw (*Corvus monedula spermologus*) | |
| | Rook (*Corvus frugilegus frugilegus*) | |
| | Carrion Crow (*Corvus corone corone*) | |
| | Hooded Crow (*Corvus corone cornix*) | |
| | Raven (*Corvus corax corax*) | |
| Family | *Bombycillidae* | |
| Subfamily | *Bombycillinae* | |
| Species | Bohemian Waxwing (*Bombycilla garrulus garrulus*) | |
| Family | *Cinclidae* | |
| Species | Dipper (*Cinclus cinclus cinclus*) | |
| | Black-bellied Water Ouzel (*Cinclus cinclus aquaticus*) | |
| Family | *Troglodytidae* | |
| Species | Wren (*Troglodytes troglodytes troglodytes*) | |
| Family | *Prunellidae* | |
| Species | Alpine Accentor (*Prunella collaris collaris*) | |
| | Dunnock (*Prunella modularis modularis*) | |
| Family | *Muscicapidae* | |
| Subfamily | *Muscicapinae* | |
| Species | Pied Flycatcher (*Ficedula hypoleuca hypoleuca*) | |
| | White-collared Flycatcher (*Ficedula albicollis albicollis*) | |
| | Red-breasted Flycatcher (*Ficedula parva parva*) | |
| | Spotted Flycatcher (*Muscicapa striata striata*) | |
| Family | *Sylviidae* | |
| Subfamily | *Sylviinae* | |
| Species | Savi's Warbler (*Locustella luscinioides luscinioides*) | |
| | Grasshopper Warbler (*Locustella naevia naevia*) | |
| | Aquatic Warbler (*Acrocephalus paludicola*) | |
| | Sedge Warbler (*Acrocephalus schoenobaenus*) | |
| | Marsh Warbler (*Acrocephalus palustris*) | |
| | Reed Warbler (*Acrocephalus scirpaceus scirpaceus*) | |
| | Great Reed Warbler (*Acrocephalus arundinaceus arundinaceus*) | |
| | Melodious Warbler (*Hippolais polyglotta*) | |
| | Orphean Warbler (*Sylvia hortensis hortensis*) | |
| | Garden Warbler (*Sylvia borin borin*) | |
| | Blackcap (*Sylvia atricapilla atricapilla*) | |
| | Whitethroat (*Sylvia communis communis*) | |
| | Lesser Whitethroat (*Sylvia curruca curruca*) | |
| | Dartford Warbler (*Sylvia undata undata*) | |

| | | |
|---|---|---|
| | Willow Warbler (*Phylloscopus trochilus trochilus*) | |
| | Chiffchaff (*Phylloscopus collybita collybita*) | |
| | Wood Warbler (*Phylloscopus sibilatrix*) | |
| | Yellow-browed Warbler (*Phylloscopus inornatus inornatus*) | |
| Subfamily | *Regulinae* | |
| Species | Goldcrest (*Regulus regulus regulus*) | |
| | Firecrest (*Regulus ignicapillus ignicapillus*) | |
| Family | *Turdidae* | |
| Species | Whinchat (*Saxicola rubetra*) | |
| | Stonechat (*Saxicola torquata rubicola*) | |
| | Wheatear (*Oenanthe oenanthe oenanthe*) | |
| | Rufous Warbler (*Cercotrichas galactotes galactotes*) | |
| | Rock Thrush (*Monticola saxatilis*) | |
| | Blue Rock Thrush (*Monticola solitarius solitarius*) | |
| | Black Redstart (*Phoenicurus ochruros gibraltariensis*) | |
| | Redstart (*Phoenicurus phoenicurus phoenicurus*) | |
| | Robin (*Erithacus rubecula rubecula*) | |
| | Nightingale (*Luscinia megarhynchos megarhynchos*) | |
| | White-throated Bluebreast (*Luscinia svecica cyanecula*) | |
| | Red-throated Bluebreast (*Luscinia svecica svecica*) | |
| | Black-throated Thrush (*Turdus ruficollis atrogularis*) | |
| | Fieldfare (*Turdus pilaris*) | |
| | Ring Ouzel (*Turdus torquatus torquatus*) | |
| | Blackbird (*Turdus merula merula*) | |
| | Siberian Thrush (*Turdus sibiricus sibiricus*) | |
| | Redwing (*Turdus iliacus iliacus*) | |
| | Song Thrush (*Turdus philomelos philomelos*) | |
| | Mistle Thrush (*Turdus viscivorus viscivorus*) | |
| | Golden Thrush (*Zoothera dauma aurea*) | |
| Family | *Timaliidae* | |
| Subfamily | *Panurinae* | |
| Species | Bearded Tit (*Panurus biarmicus biarmicus*) | |
| Family | *Aegithalidae* | |
| Species | Long-tailed Tit (*Aegithalos caudatus europaeus*) | |
| Family | *Paridae* | |
| Species | Marsh Tit (*Parus palustris palustris*) | |
| | Crested Tit (*Parus cristatus cristatus*) | |
| | Coal Tit (*Parus ater ater*) | |
| | Blue Tit (*Parus caeruleus caeruleus*) | |
| | Great Tit (*Parus major major*) | |
| Family | *Sittidae* | |
| Subfamily | *Sittinae* | |
| Species | Nuthatch (*Sitta europaea europaea*) | |
| Family | *Certhiidae* | |
| Species | Treecreeper (*Certhia familiaris macrodactyla*) | |
| Family | *Ploceidae* | |
| Subfamily | *Passerinae* | |
| Species | House Sparrow (*Passer domesticus domesticus*) | |
| | Tree Sparrow (*Passer montanus montanus*) | |
| Family | *Fringillidae* | |
| Subfamily | *Fringillinae* | |
| Species | Chaffinch (*Fringilla coelebs coelebs*) | |
| | Brambling (*Fringilla montifringilla*) | |
| Subfamily | *Carduelinae* | |
| Species | Serin (*Serinus serinus*) | |
| | Greenfinch (*Carduelis chloris aurantiiventris*) | |
| | Siskin (*Carduelis spinus*) | |
| | Goldfinch (*Carduelis carduelis carduelis*) | |
| | Twite (*Acanthis flavirostris flavirostris*) | |
| | Linnet (*Acanthis cannabina cannabina*) | |
| | Redpoll (*Acanthis flammea flammea*) | |
| | Lesser Redpoll (*Acanthis flammea cabaret*) | |
| | Scarlet Grosbeak (*Carpodacus erythrinus erythrinus*) | |
| | Pine Grosbeak (*Pinicola enucleator enucleator*) | |
| | Parrot Crossbill (*Loxia pytyopsittacus*) | |
| | Crossbill (*Loxia curvirostra curvirostra*) | |
| | Two-barred Crossbill (*Loxia leucoptera bifasciata*) | |
| | American White-winged Crossbill (*Loxia leucoptera americana*) | |
| | Bullfinch (*Pyrrhula pyrrhula europaea*) | |
| | Hawfinch (*Coccothraustes coccothraustes coccothraustes*) | |
| Family | *Emberizidae* | |
| Species | Corn Bunting (*Emberiza calandra calandra*) | |
| | Yellow Bunting (*Emberiza citrinella citrinella*) | |
| | Ortolan Bunting (*Emberiza hortulana*) | |
| | Cirl Bunting (*Emberiza cirlus cirlus*) | |
| | Dwarf Bunting (*Emberiza pusilla*) | |
| | Rustic Bunting (*Emberiza rustica rustica*) | |
| | Black-headed Bunting (*Emberiza melanocephala*) | |
| | Reed Bunting (*Emberiza schoeniclus schoeniclus*) | |
| | Lapland Bunting (*Calcarius lapponicus lapponicus*) | |
| | Snow Bunting (*Plectrophenax nivalis nivalis*) | |

# Index of illustrations

*Acanthis cannabina c.*, 122
   *flammea cabaret*, 124
   *flammea f.*, 123
   *flavirostris f.*, 123
Accentor,
   Alpine, 83
*Accipiter gentilis g.*, 38
   *nisus n.*, 38
*Accipitridae*, 34–38, 45–47
*Acrocephalus arundinaceus a.*, 92
   *paludicola*, 94
   *palustris*, 93
   *schoenobaenus*, 94
   *scirpaceus s.*, 93
*Aegithalidae*, 69, 70
*Aegithalos caudatus europaeus*, 69, 70
*Aegolius funereus f.*, 52
*Alauda arvensis a.*, 104
*Alaudidae*, 104, 106–8
*Alca impennis*, 210
   *torda t.*, 211
*Alcedinidae*, 60
*Alcedo atthis ispida*, 60
*Alcidae*, 210–13
*Alectoris rufa r.*, 148
*Anas acuta a.*, 196
   *clypeata*, 194
   *crecca c.*, 195
   *penelope*, 194
   *querquedula*, 196
   *platyrhynchos p.*, 195
   *strepera s.*, 197
*Anatidae* 188–206
*Anser albifrons a.*, 189
   *anser a.*, 188
   *fabalis brachyrhynchus*, 189
   *fabalis f.*, 188
*Anseriformes* 188–206
*Anthus campestris c.*, 102
   *cervinus*, 103
   *novaeseelandiae richardi*, 101
   *pratensis p.*, 105
   *spinoletta littoralis*, 102
   *spinoletta s.*, 103
   *trivialis t.*, 105
*Apodidae*, 57
*Apodiformes*, 57
*Apodinae*, 57
*Apus apus a.*, 57
   *melba m.*, 57
*Aquila chrysaëtos c.*, 34
   *pomarina p.*, 35
*Ardea cinerea c.*, 147
   *purpurea p.*, 150
*Ardeidae*, 147, 150–54
*Ardeola ralloides*, 152
*Arenaria interpres i.*, 170
*Asio flammeus f.*, 50
   *otus o.*, 50
*Athene noctua n.*, 53
Auk,
   Great, 210
   Little, 212
Avocet, 166
*Aythya ferina*, 197
   *fuligula*, 199
   *marila m.*, 199
   *nyroca*, 198

*Bartramia longicauda*, 171

Bee-eater, 60
Bittern, 153
   American, 153
   Little, 154
Blackbird, 74
Blackcap, 86
Bluebreast,
   Red-throated, 80
   White-throated, 81
*Bombycilla garrulus g.*, 66
*Bombycillidae*, 66
*Bombycillinae*, 66
*Botaurus lentiginosus l.*, 153
   *stellaris*, 153
Brambling, 115
*Branta bernicla b.*, 191
   *leucopsis*, 190
   *ruficollis*, 190
*Bubo bubo b.*, 49
*Bubulcus ibis i.*, 151
*Bucephala clangula c.*, 203
Bullfinch, 118, 119
Bunting,
   Black-headed, 111
   Cirl, 109
   Corn, 110
   Dwarf, 110
   Lapland, 112
   Ortolan, 111
   Reed, 112
   Rustic, 109
   Snow, 114
   Yellow, 108
*Burhinidae*, 157
*Burhinus oedicnemus o.*, 157
Bustard,
   Great, 146
   Little, 146
*Buteo buteo b.*, 37
   *lagopus l.*, 36
Buzzard,
   Common, 37
   Honey, 37
   Rough-legged, 36

*Calandrella cinerea brachydactyla*, 108
*Calcarius lapponicus l.*, 112
*Calidris alba*, 173
   *alpina a.*, 174, 175
   *canutus c.*, 172
   *ferruginea*, 174
   *fuscicollis*, 175
   *maritima*, 177
   *melanotos*, 173
   *minuta*, 176
   *minutilla*, 177
   *temminckii*, 176
Capercaillie, 142
*Caprimulgidae*, 56
*Caprimulgiformes*, 56
*Caprimulgus europaeus e.*, 56
   *ruficollis r.*, 56
*Carduelinae*, 116–24
*Carduelis carduelis c.*, 116
   *chloris aurantiiventris*, 117
   *spinus*, 116
*Carpodacus erythrinus e.*, 119
*Cepphus grylle*, 212
*Cercotrichas galactotes g.*, 82
*Certhia familiaris macrodactyla*, 88

*Certhiidae*, 88
Chaffinch, 115
*Charadriidae*, 156–61, 170
*Charadriiformes*, 156–81, 210–13, 215–28
*Charadrius alexandrinus a.*, 160
   *dubius curonicus*, 161
   *hiaticula h.*, 160
Chiffchaff, 89
*Chlidonias hybrida h.*, 226
   *leucopterus*, 226
   *niger n.*, 225
Chough, 129
*Ciconia ciconia c.*, 155
   *nigra*, 155
*Ciconiidae*, 155
*Ciconiiformes*, 147, 150–55
*Cinclidae*, 76, 77
*Cinclus cinclus aquaticus*, 77
   *cinclus c.*, 76
*Circus aeruginosus a.*, 46
   *cyaneus c.*, 47
   *pygargus*, 47
*Clamator glandarius*, 133
*Clangula hyemalis*, 204
*Coccothraustes coccothraustes c.*, 118
*Columba livia l.*, 141
   *oenas o.*, 140
   *palumbus p.*, 140
*Columbidae*, 140, 141
*Columbiformes*, 140, 141, 145
Coot, 182
*Coracias garrulus g.*, 61
*Coraciidae*, 61
*Coraciiformes*, 60, 61
*Coraciinae*, 61
Cormorant, 214
*Corvidae*, 127–32
*Corvus corax c.*, 127
   *corone cornix*, 128
   *corone c.*, 127
   *frugilegus f.*, 128
   *monedula spermologus*, 129
*Coturnix coturnix c.*, 149
Courser,
   Cream-coloured, 162
Crake,
   Baillon's, 184
   Corn, 183
   Little, 185
   Spotted, 184
Crane, 147
*Crex crex*, 183
Crossbill, 120
   American White-winged, 122
   Parrot, 121
   Two-barred, 121
Crow,
   Carrion, 127
   Hooded, 128
Cuckoo, 132, 133
   Great Spotted, 133
*Cuculidae*, 132, 133
*Cuculiformes*, 132, 133
*Cuculinae*, 132, 133
*Cuculus canorus c.*, 132, 133
Curlew, 164
   Stone, 157
*Cursorius cursor c.*, 162
*Cygnus bewickii*, 192
*Cygnus cygnus*, 192

*Cygnus olor*, 191

*Delichon urbica u.*, 58
*Dendrocopos leucotos l.*, 134
   *major m.*, 134
   *minor buturlini*, 135
Dipper, 76
Diver,
   Black-throated, 209
   Great Northern, 209
   Red-throated, 210
Dotterel, 161
Dove,
   Stock, 140
   Turtle, 141
*Dryocopus martius m.*, 135
Duck,
   Harlequin, 203
   Long-tailed, 204
   Red-crested, 198
   Scaup, 199
   Shoveller, 194
   Tufted, 199
Dunlin, 174, 175
Dunnock, 83

Eagle,
   Golden, 34
   Lesser Spotted, 35
   White-tailed, 35
Egret,
   Cattle, 151
   Great White, 150
   Little, 151
*Egretta alba a.*, 150
   *garzetta g.*, 151
Eider,
   Common, 200
   King, 201
   Steller's, 200
*Emberiza calandra c.*, 110
   *cirlus c.*, 109
   *citrinella c.*, 108
   *hortulana*, 111
   *melanocephala*, 111
   *pusilla*, 110
   *rustica r.*, 109
   *schoeniclus s.*, 112
*Emberizidae*, 108–12, 114
*Eremophila alpestris flava*, 106
*Erithacus rubecula r.*, 80
*Eudromias morinellus*, 161

*Falco columbarius aesalon*, 43
   *peregrinus p.*, 42
   *rusticolus candicans*, 40, 41
   *rusticolus islandicus*, 39, 43
   *rusticolus r.*, 41
   *subbuteo s.*, 42
   *tinnunculus t.*, 44
   *vespertinus v.*, 44
Falcon,
   Peregrine, 42
   Red-footed, 44
*Falconidae*, 38, 40–44
*Falconiformes*, 34–38, 40–47
*Ficedula albicollis a.*, 64
   *hypoleuca h.*, 64

*parva p.*, 65
Fieldfare, 73
Firecrest, 91
Flycatcher,
    Pied, 64
    Red-breasted, 65
    Spotted, 65
    White-collared, 64
*Fratercula arctica grabae*, 213
*Fringilla coelebs c.*, 115
    *montifringilla*, 115
*Fringillidae*, 115–24
*Fringillinae*, 115
*Fulica atra a.*, 182
Fulmar,
    Northern, 229
*Fulmarus glacialis*, 229

Gadwall, 197
*Galerida cristata c.*, 106
*Galliformes*, 142–45, 148, 149
*Gallinago gallinago g.*, 179
    *media*, 179
*Gallinula chloropus c.*, 182
Gannet, 215
Garganey, 196
*Garrulus glandarius g.*, 130
*Gavia arctica a.*, 209
    *immer*, 209
    *stellata s.*, 210
*Gaviidae*, 209, 210
*Gaviiformes*, 209, 210
*Gelochelidon nilotica n.*, 225
*Glareola pratincola p.*, 163
*Glareolidae*, 162, 163
Godwit,
    Bar-tailed, 165
    Black-tailed, 165
Goldcrest, 91
Goldeneye, 203
Goldfinch, 116
Goshawk, 38
Goose,
    Barnacle, 190
    Bean, 188
    Brent, 191
    Grey Lag, 188
    Pink-footed, 198
    Red-breasted, 190
    White-fronted, 189
Goosander, 204
Grebe,
    Black-necked, 208
    Great-crested, 206
    Horned, 207
    Little, 208
    Red-necked, 207
Greenfinch, 117
Greenshank, 166
Grosbeak,
    Pine, 120
    Scarlet, 119
Grouse,
    Black, 142
    Red, 143
*Gruidae*, 147
*Gruiformes*, 146, 147, 149, 182–85
*Grus grus g.*, 147
Guillemot,
    Black, 212
    Common, 211
Gull,
    Black-headed, 220
    Bonaparte's, 220
    Common, 218
    Glaucous, 216
    Great Black-backed, 215
    Herring, 217
    Iceland, 217
    Ivory, 219
    Little, 221
    Lesser Black-backed, 216
    Ross's, 219

Sabine's, 221
Gyrfalcon, 41
    Greenland, 40, 41
    Icelandic, 39, 43

*Haematopodidae*, 162
*Haematopus ostralegus o.*, 162
*Haliaëtus albicilla*, 35
Harrier,
    Hen, 47
    Marsh, 46
    Montagu's, 47
Hawfinch, 118
Heron,
    Grey, 147
    Night, 152
    Purple, 150
    Squacco, 152
*Himantopus himantopus h.*, 156
*Hippolais polyglotta*, 92
*Hirundinidae*, 58, 59
*Hirundo rustica r.*, 58
*Histrionicus histrionicus*, 203
Hobby, 42
Hoopoe, 61
*Hydrobates pelagicus*, 231
*Hydrobatidae*, 230, 231
*Hydroprogne tschegrava*, 222

Ibis,
    Glossy, 163
*Ixobrychus minutus m.*, 154

Jackdaw, 129
Jay, 130
*Jynginae*, 137
*Jynx torquilla t.*, 137

Kestrel, 44
Kingfisher, 60
Kite,
    Black, 45
    Red, 45
Kittiwake, 218
Knot,
    Red, 172

*Lagopus lagopus scoticus*, 143
    *mutus helveticus*, 143, 144
*Laniidae*, 62, 63
*Lanius collurio c.*, 63
    *excubitor e.*, 62
    *minor m.*, 62
    *senator s.*, 63
Lapwing, 156
*Laridae*, 215–28
*Larinae*, 215–21
Lark,
    Calandra, 107
    Crested, 106
    Horned, 106
    Short-toed, 108
    Sky, 104
    White-winged, 107
    Wood, 104
*Larus argentatus a.*, 217
    *canus c.*, 218
    *fuscus f.*, 215
    *glaucoides g.*, 217
    *hyperboreus h.*, 216
    *marinus*, 215
    *minutus*, 221
    *philadelphia*, 220
    *ridibundus*, 220
*Limosa lapponica l.*, 165
    *limosa l.*, 165
*Limnodromus scolapaceus*, 178
Linnet, 122
*Locustella luscinioides l.*, 95

*naevia n.*, 95
*Loxia curvirostra c.*, 120
    *leucoptera americana*, 122
    *leucoptera bifasciata*, 121
    *pytyopsittacus*, 121
*Lullula arborea a.*, 104
*Luscinia megarhynchos m.*, 84
    *svecica cyanecula*, 81
    *svecica s.*, 80
*Lymnocryptes minimus*, 180
*Lyrurus tetrix t.*, 142

Magpie, 130
Mallard, 195
Martin,
    House, 58
    Sand, 59
*Melanitta fusca f.*, 202
    *nigra n.*, 201
    *perspicillata*, 202
*Melanocorypha calandra c.*, 107
    *leucoptera*, 107
Merganser,
    Hooded, 205
    Red-breasted, 205
*Mergus albellus*, 206
    *cucullatus*, 205
    *merganser m.*, 204
    *serrator*, 205
Merlin, 43
*Meropidae*, 60
*Merops apiaster*, 60
*Milvus migrans m.*, 45
    *milvus m.*, 45
*Monticola saxatilis*, 78
    *solitarius s.*, 77
Moorhen, 182
*Motacilla alba a.*, 98
    *alba yarrellii*, 98
    *cinerea c.*, 100, 101
    *flava cinereocapilla*, 100
    *flava f.*, 99
    *flava flavissima*, 99
    *flava iberiae*, 100
*Motacillidae*, 98–103, 105
*Muscicapa striata s.*, 65
*Muscicapidae*, 64, 65
*Muscicapinae*, 64, 65

*Neophron percnopterus p.*, 34
*Netta rufina*, 198
Nightingale, 84
Nightjar, 56
    Red-necked, 56
*Nucifraga caryocatactes c.*, 131, 132
Nutcracker, 131, 132
Nuthatch, 66
*Nyctea scandiaca*, 51
*Nycticorax nycticorax n*, 152
*Numenius arquata a.*, 164
    *phaeopus p.*, 164

*Oceanodroma leucorhoa l.*, 230
*Oenanthe oenanthe o.*, 78
Oriole,
    Golden, 71
*Oriolidae*, 71
*Oriolus oriolus o.*, 71
Osprey, 36
*Otididae*, 146
*Otis tarda t.*, 146
    *tetrax t.*, 146
*Otus scops s.*, 51
Ouzel,
    Black-bellied Water, 77
    Ring, 75
Owl,
    Barn, 48
    Eagle, 49
    Hawk, 52
    Little, 53

    Long-eared, 50
    Scops, 51
    Short-eared, 50
    Snowy, 51
    Tawny, 48
    Tengmalm's, 52
Oystercatcher, 162

*Pagophila eburnea*, 219
*Pandion haliaëtus h.*, 36
*Pandionidae*, 36
*Panurinae*, 70
*Panurus biarmicus b.*, 70
*Paridae*, 67–69
Partridge,
    Grey, 148
    Red-legged, 148
*Parus ater a.*, 68
    *caeruleus c.*, 67
    *cristatus c.*, 68
    *major m.*, 67
    *palustris p.*, 69
*Passer domesticus d.*, 113
    *montanus m.*, 114
*Passeriformes*, 58, 59, 62–95, 98–132
*Passerinae*, 113, 114
Pastor,
    Rose-coloured, 126
*Pelecaniformes*, 214, 215
*Perdix perdix italica*, 148
*Pernis apivorus*, 37
Petrel,
    Leach's, 230
    Storm, 231
*Phalacrocoracidae*, 214
*Phalacrocorax aristotelis a.*, 214
    *carbo c.*, 214
Phalarope,
    Grey, 180, 181
    Red-necked, 181
*Phalaropodidae*, 180, 181
*Phalaropus fulicarius*, 180, 181
    *lobatus*, 181
*Phasianidae*, 145, 148, 149
*Phasianus colchicus c.*, 145
Pheasant, 145
*Philomachus pugnax*, 170, 171
*Phoenicurus ochruros gibralteriensis*, 82
    *phoenicurus p.*, 81
*Phylloscopus collybita c.*, 89
    *inornatus i.*, 90
    *sibilatrix*, 90
    *trochilus t.*, 89
*Pica pica p.*, 130
*Picidae*, 134–37
*Piciformes*, 134–37
*Picinae*, 134–36
*Picus viridis pronus*, 136
Pigeon,
    Rock, 141
    Wood, 140
*Pinicola enucleator e.*, 120
Pintail, 196
Pipit,
    Meadow, 105
    Red-throated, 103
    Richard's, 101
    Rock, 102
    Tawny, 102
    Tree, 105
    Water, 103
*Platalea leucorodia l.*, 154
*Plectrophenax nivalis n.*, 114
*Plegadis falcinellus*, 163
*Ploceidae*, 113, 114
*Plotus alle a.*, 212
Plover,
    Black-bellied, 157, 158
    Golden, 158, 159
    Kentish, 160
    Little Ringed, 161
    Ringed, 160
*Pluvialis apricaria a.*, 158, 159

*squatarola*, 157, 158
Pochard, 197
 White-eyed, 198
*Podiceps auritus a.*, 207
 *cristatus c.*, 206
 *grisegena g.*, 207
 *nigricollis n.*, 208
 *ruficollis r.*, 208
*Podicipedidae*, 206–8
*Podicipediformes*, 206–8
*Polysticta stelleri*, 200
*Porzana parva*, 185
 *porzana*, 184
 *pusilla intermedia*, 184
Pratincole, 163
*Procellariidae*, 229, 230
*Procellariiformes*, 229–31
*Prunella collaris c.*, 83
 *modularis m.*, 83
*Prunellidae*, 83
Ptarmigan,
 Rock, 143, 144
*Pteroclidae*, 145
Puffin, 213
*Puffinus assimilis baroli*, 230
*Puffinus puffinus yelkouan*, 229
*Pyrrhocorax pyrrhocorax erythrorhamphus*, 129
*Pyrrhula pyrrhula europaea*, 118, 119

Quail,
 Common, 149
 Little Button, 149

Rail,
 Water, 183
*Rallidae*, 182–85
*Rallus aquaticus a.*, 183
Raven, 127
Razorbill, 211
*Recurvirostra avosetta a.*, 166
*Recurvirostridae*, 156
Redpoll, 123
 Lesser, 124
Redshank, 167
 Spotted, 167
Redstart, 81
 Black, 82
Redwing, 73
*Regulinae*, 91
*Regulus ignicapillus i.*, 91
 *regulus r.*, 91
*Rhodostethia rosea*, 219
*Riparia riparia r.*, 58, 59
*Rissa tridactyla*, 218
Robin, 80
Roller, 61
Rook, 128
Ruff, 170, 171

Sanderling, 173
Sandgrouse,
 Pallas's, 145
Sandpiper,
 Buff-breasted, 172
 Common, 169
 Curlew, 174
 Green, 168
 Least, 177
 Pectoral, 173
 Purple, 177
 Spotted, 169
 Upland, 171
 White-rumped, 175
 Wood, 168
*Saxicola rubetra*, 79
 *torquata rubicola*, 79
*Scolopacidae*, 164–80
*Scolopax rusticola*, 178
Scoter,
 Black, 201

Surf, 202
 Velvet, 202
Serin, 117
*Serinus serinus*, 117
Shag, 214
Shearwater,
 Little, 230
 Manx, 229
Shelduck, 193
 Ruddy, 193
Shrike,
 Great Grey, 62
 Lesser Grey, 62
 Red-backed, 63
 Woodchat, 63
Siskin, 116
*Sitta europaea e.*, 66
*Sittidae*, 66
*Sittinae*, 66
Skua,
 Arctic, 228
 Great, 227
 Long-tailed, 228
 Pomathorine, 227
Smew, 206
Snipe,
 Brown, 178
 Common, 179
 Great, 179
 Jack, 180
*Somateria mollissima m.*, 200
 *spectabilis*, 201
Sparrow,
 House, 113
 Tree, 114
Sparrowhawk, 38
Spoonbill, 154
Starling, 124, 125
*Stercorarinae*, 227, 228
*Stercorarius longicaudus*, 228
 *parasiticus*, 228
 *pomarinus*, 227
 *skua s.*, 227
*Sterna albifrons a.*, 224
 *dougallii d*, 223
 *hirundo h.*, 223
 *paradisea*, 224
 *sandvicensis s.*, 222
*Sterninae*, 222–26
Stilt,
 Black-winged, 156
Stint,
 Little, 176
 Temminck's, 176
Stonechat, 79
Stork,
 Black, 155
 White, 155
*Streptopelia turtur t.*, 141
*Strigidae*, 48–53
*Strigiformes*, 48–53
*Striginae*, 48–53
*Strix aluco a.*, 48
*Sturnidae*, 124–26
*Sturnus roseus*, 126
 *vulgaris v.*, 124, 125
*Sula bassana b.*, 215
*Sulidae*, 215
*Surnia ulula*, 52
Swan,
 Bewick's, 192
 Mute, 191
 Whooper, 192
Swallow,
 Barn, 58
Swift, 57
 Alpine, 57
*Sylvia atricapilla a.*, 86
 *borin b.*, 87
 *communis c.*, 84
 *curruca c.*, 86
 *hortensis h.*, 87
 *undata u.*, 85
*Sylviidae*, 84–95

*Sylviinae*, 84–95
*Syrrhaptes paradoxus*, 145

*Tadorna ferruginea*, 193
 *tadorna*, 193
Teal, 195
Tern,
 Arctic, 224
 Black, 225
 Caspian, 222
 Common, 223
 Gull-billed, 224
 Little, 224
 Roseate, 223
 Sandwich, 222
 Whiskered, 226
 White-winged Black, 226
*Tetraonidae*, 142–44
*Tetrao urogallus u.*, 142
*Threskiornithidae*, 154, 163
Thrush,
 Black-throated, 74
 Blue Rock, 77
 Golden, 75
 Mistle, 72
 Rock, 78
 Siberian, 76
 Song, 72
*Timaliidae*, 70
Tit,
 Bearded, 70
 Blue, 67
 Coal, 68
 Crested, 68
 Great, 67
 Long-tailed, 69, 70
 Marsh, 69
Treecreeper, 88
*Tringa erythropus*, 167
 *glareola*, 168
 *hypoleucos*, 169
 *macularia*, 169
 *nebularia*, 166
 *ochropus*, 168
 *totanus t.*, 167
*Troglodytes troglodytes t.*, 88
*Troglodytidae*, 88
*Tryngites subruficollis*, 172
*Turdidae*, 72–82, 84
*Turdus iliacus i.*, 73
 *merula m.*, 74
 *philomelos p.*, 72
 *pilaris*, 73
 *ruficollis atrogularis*, 74
 *sibiricus s.*, 76
 *torquatus t.*, 75
 *viscivorus v.*, 72
*Turnicidae*, 149
*Turnix sylvatica s.*, 149
Turnstone, 170
Twite, 123
*Tyto alba a.*, 48
*Tytoninae*, 48

*Upupa epops e.*, 61
*Upupidae*, 61
*Upupinae*, 61
*Uria aalge albionis*, 211

*Vanellus vanellus*, 156
Vulture,
 Egyptian 34

Wagtail,
 Grey, 100, 101
 Grey-capped, 100
 Grey-headed, 99
 Pied, 98
 Spanish, 100
 White, 98

Yellow, 99
Warbler,
 Aquatic, 94
 Dartford, 85
 Garden, 87
 Grasshopper, 95
 Great Reed, 92
 Marsh, 93
 Melodious, 92
 Orphean, 87
 Reed, 93
 Rufous, 82
 Savi's, 95
 Sedge, 94
 Yellow-browed, 90
 Willow, 89
 Wood, 90
Waxwing,
 Bohemian, 66
Wheatear, 78
Whimbrel, 164
Whinchat, 79
Whitethroat, 84
 Lesser, 86
Widgeon, 194
Woodcock, 178
Woodpecker,
 Great Black, 135
 Great Spotted, 134
 Green, 136
 Lesser Spotted, 135
 White-backed, 134
Wren, 88
Wryneck, 137

*Xema sabini*, 221

*Zoothera dauma aurea*, 75

# Bibliography

## Original Editions of the Works of John Gould

*A Century of Birds from the Himalaya Mountains*, London 1831 and 1832. Eighty colour lithographs. Drawings and lithographs by Elizabeth Gould from sketches by John Gould.

*The Birds of Europe*, London 1832–37. Four hundred and forty-eight colour lithographs. Drawings and lithographs by Elizabeth Gould and Edward Lear from sketches and drawings by John Gould; coloured by George Bayfield and Elizabeth Gould.

*A Monograph of the Ramphastidae, or Family of Toucans*, London 1834 and 1835. Thirty-four lithographs, of which 33 in colour. 1855 supplement with 21 lithographs. Second edition 1854 with 52 lithographs, of which 51 in colour. Drawings and lithographs by Elizabeth Gould, John Gould, Edward Lear, Henry Constantine Richter (for the supplement), Georg Scharf.

*A Monograph of the Trogonidae, or Family of Trogons*, London 1838. Thirty-six colour lithographs. Second edition 1858–75 with 47 plates. Drawings and lithographs by Elizabeth Gould, John Gould, Edward Lear.

*Icones avium, or figures and descriptions of new and interesting species of birds from various parts of the globe*, London 1837–38. Eighteen colour lithographs. Drawings and lithographs by Elizabeth Gould and John Gould.

*The Birds of Australia and the adjacent islands*, London 1837–38. Twenty colour lithographs. Drawings and lithographs by Elizabeth Gould and John Gould.

*The Zoology of the Voyage of H.M.S. Beagle, under the command of Captain Fitzroy . . . 1832–36. Published with the approval of the Lords Commissioners of Her Majesty's Treasury. Edited and superintended by Charles Darwin. Part III. Birds, described by John Gould, with a notice of their habits and ranges, by Charles Darwin, and with an anatomical appendix, by T. C. Eyton*, London 1838–41. Fifty colour lithographs. Drawings and lithographs by Elizabeth Gould from sketches by John Gould.

*The Birds of Australia*, London 1840–48. Six hundred colour lithographs. Supplement 1851–69 with 81 colour lithographs. Drawings and lithographs by Elizabeth Gould, John Gould, Henry Constantine Richter.

*A Monograph of the Macropodidae, or Family of Kangaroos*, London 1841–42. Thirty colour lithographs. Drawings and lithographs by Henry Constantine Richter.

*The Zoology of the Voyage of H.M.S. Sulphur, under the command of Captain Sir Edward Belcher . . . 1836–42. Published under the authority of the Lords Commissioners of the Admiralty. Edited and superintended by Richard Brinsley Hinds. Birds, by John Gould*, London 1843–44. Sixteen colour lithographs. Drawings by John Gould, Benjamin Waterhouse Hawkins. Lithographs by Benjamin Waterhouse Hawkins.

*A Monograph of the Odontophorinae, or Partridges of America*, London 1844–50. Thirty-two colour lithographs. Drawings and lithographs by John Gould and Henry Constantine Richter.

*The Mammals of Australia*, London 1845–63. One hundred and eighty-two colour lithographs. Drawings and lithographs by John Gould, Henry Constantine Richter, Joseph Wolf.

*A Monograph of the Trochilidae, or Family of Humming-birds*, London 1849–61. Three hundred and sixty colour lithographs. Supplement 1880–87 with 58 colour lithographs. Drawings and lithographs by John Gould, William Hart (for the supplement), Henry Constantine Richter; coloured by George Bayfield.

*The Birds of Asia*, London 1850–83. Five hundred and thirty colour lithographs. Drawings and lithographs by John Gould, William Hart, Henry Constantine Richter, Joseph Wolf.

*The Birds of New Guinea and the adjacent Papuan islands, including many new species recently discovered in Australia*, London 1875–88. Three hundred colour lithographs. Drawings and lithographs by John Gould and William Hart.

## Further Reading

Anker, J. *Bird Books and Bird Art*, Copenhagen 1938

Bannerman, D. A. and Lodge, G. E. *The Birds of the British Isles* (12 vols.), London 1953–63

Barret, C. L. *The Bird Man: A sketch of the life of John Gould*, Melbourne–Sydney 1938

Benson, S. V. *The Observer's Book of British Birds*, London 1965

Bowdler Sharpe, R. *An Analytical Index to the Works of the Late John Gould, F.R.S.*, London 1893

British Ornithologists' Union *Check-list of the Birds of Great Britain and Ireland*, London 1952

Bruun, B. *The Concise Encyclopedia of Birds*, London 1974

Bruun, B. *The Hamlyn Guide to Birds of Britain and Europe*, London 1970

Chisholm, A. H. *The Story of Mrs Elizabeth Gould*, Melbourne 1944

Curry-Lindahl, K. (ed.) *et al. Våra faglar i Norden* (4 vols.) Stockholm 1959

Cäläne, H. *Was fliegt denn da?*, Stuttgart 1958

Géroudet, P. *La Vie des Oiseaux* (6 vols.), Neuchâtel and Paris 1947–57

Glutz von Blotzheim, U. N. *et al. Handbuch der Vögel Mitteleuropas*, Frankfurt 1966

Gruson, E. S. *A Check-list of the Birds of the World*, London 1976

Hollom, P. A. D. *The Popular Handbook of British Birds*, London 1962

Hollom, P. A. D. *The Popular Handbook of Rarer British Birds*, London 1960

Jackson, C. E. *Bird Illustrators. Some Artists in Early Lithography*, London 1975

Makatsch, W. *Die Vögel Europas*, Leipzig 1966

Makatsch, W. *Verzeichnis der Vögel Deutschlands*, Radebeul and Berlin 1957

Maynaud, N. *et al. Inventaire des Oiseaux de France*, Paris 1936

McEvey, A. *John Gould's Contribution to British Art*, Sydney 1973

Niethammer, G. *Handbuch der Deutschen Vogelkunde* (3 vols.), Leipzig 1937–42

Niethammer, G. *Handbuch der Vögel Mitteleuropas*, vol. I, Frankfurt 1966

Niethammer, G. *et al. Die Vögel Deutschlands: Artenliste*, Frankfurt 1964

Nissen, C. *Die Illustrierten Vögelbücher*, Stuttgart 1953

Nissen, C. *Die Zoologische Buchillustration*, Stuttgart 1969–78

Palmer, A. H. *The Life of Joseph Wolf*, London 1895

Peterson, R. *et al. Die Vögel Europas*, Berlin 1965

Ridgway, J. L. *Scientific Illustration*, Stanford University Press (California) 1938

Salvadori, T. *Fauna d'Italia*, Milan 1872

Salvadori, T. *et al. Della vita e delle opere dell'ornitologo inglese John Gould*, Turin 1881

Scherren, H. *The Zoological Society of London. A Sketch of its Foundation and Development*, London 1905

Scott, P. *A Coloured Key to the Wildfowl of the World*, London 1968

Sharrock, J. T. R. *The Atlas of Breeding Birds in Britain and Ireland*, London 1976

Stresemann, E. *Die Entwicklung der Ornithologie*, Berlin 1951

Thomson, A. Landsborough *A New Dictionary of Birds*, London 1964

Timmerman, G. *Die Vögel Islands*, Reykjavik 1938–49

Verheyen, R. *La Vie des Oiseaux* (8 vols.), Brussels 1943–51

Voous, K. H. *Atlas of European Birds*, London 1960

Voous, K. H. *Die Vogelwelt Europas*, Berlin 1962

Witherby, H. F. *et al. The Handbook of British Birds* (5 vols.), London 1949